WALKER'S INSULATION TECHNIQUES AND ESTIMATING HANDBOOK

A Reference Book Setting Forth Detailed
Procedures and Cost Guidelines For
Those Involved In Estimating and
Installing Insulation

Written By
HARRY HARDENBROOK
Revised and Edited by
Gary D. Cook

FRANK R. WALKER COMPANY

PUBLISHERS
5030 N. Harlem Ave.
Chicago, Ill. 60656
Phone 312-867-7070

Every attempt has been made to make this book as accurate and authoritative as possible. We will be grateful to readers of this volume who will kindly call attention to any errors, typographical or otherwise. We also invite constructive criticism and suggestions that will make future editions of this book more complete and useful.

FRANK R. WALKER COMPANY

ISBN-0-911592-51-2

Printed in the U.S.A.

IMPORTANT

How To obtain The Best Results From The Techniques, Estimating And Cost Data in This Book

The profitibility of your business depends on (1) building a good reputation by using proven and effective insulation techniques, and (2) on the accuracy of estimating the job. YOU CANNOT BE TO CAREFUL!

This handbook provides the insulation contractor with a convenient reference addressing virtually all aspects of insulation techniques and estimating. Reference charts, maps, and tables are located throughout the book. Mastery of the techniques used in the insulation trade is built on a general understanding of the "Fundamentals" in Chapter 1 and the terms included in the "Glossary". Other chapters are subject specific, showing a variety approaches to application, installation, and estimating.

Before reading this book in depth, a quick thumb through is recommended to familiarize yourself with the location of reference material.

In compiling a book of estimating and cost data that is used throughout the world, it is impossible to quote material prices and labor costs which will apply universally. Some computation is required on the part of the reader to make this book an accurate estimating reference in your construction area.

Here is the method by which the labor figures were developed:

A standard eight (8) hour day was divided by the number of squares of material installed by each worker in that eight hour day to find the decimal fraction of an hour in which 100 sq. ft. (or cu. ft. or bd. ft. as applicable) could be installed. Example: "An applicator and assistant can install about 3600 sq. ft. of product in an 8 hour day." 8 divided by 36 (squares) = .22, therefore, each worker in the chart is shown as being able to do his part of the work of installing 100 sq. ft. in .22 of an hour, or a little less than 15 minutes.

Each worker's rate is then multiplied by the decimal fraction of an hour to determine the labor rate for each to accomplish a square, and the rate of all laborers on the job is added together to determine the total labor cost for installing each square. Thus: Carpenter at $13.35 x .22 = $2.94; Laborer at $10.60 x .22 = $2.33. $2.94 + $2.33 = $5.27 total labor cost per square.

To determine the cost per square foot, the total labor costs for an eight (8) hour day are divided by the total square feet of application during the day. Example: Carpenter at $13.35 + Laborer at $10.60 + $23.95 total labor costs per hour. The total labor cost $23.95 x 8 hours = $191.60 total labor costs per day which is divided by 3600 sq. ft. applied in a day = $0.0532 per sq. ft. (rounded off to 5¢).

In the case of the examples set forth in the product chapters, where there is a range, the average of the two figures is used. Thus, when the amount of material placed in an 8-hour day ranges from 1700–2200 sq. ft., the average is 1950 sq. ft.

In order that this data will prove to be of the utmost value to you in your business, blank rate and total tables have been left for you to insert your local wage scale.

For example on page 77:

Retrofit Industrial/Commercial Construction (roofs and ceilings). Including preparatory work, an experienced carpenter should be able to place and staple 800–1600 sq. ft. of insulation per 8-hour day at the following labor cost per 100 sq. ft.:

	Hours	Rate	Total	Rate	Total
Carpenter..................................	.66	$	$	$13.35	$8.89
Cost per sq. ft............................		. . . .	. . . .		$0.09

Now insert your local prices in the tables and you will see how accurate your estimates will be:

	Hours	Rate	Total	Rate	Total
Carpenter..................................	.66	$12.00	$7.92	$13.35	$8.89
Cost per sq. ft............................		$	$0.08	$	$0.09

The hourly rates shown herein are taken from the U. S. Department of Labor, Bureau of Labor Statistics figures as reported in publication Summary 79-8 issued June 1979 and reflect national averages (including fringe benefits) for the building trades. Space has been provided for you to insert YOUR LOCAL FIGURES for materials and labor INCLUDING FRINGE BENEFITS which then makes this book accurate for your market. You will thereby eliminate estimates which are too high or too low. Remember, however, to revise your figures as your local labor rates and material costs change.

The profitability of your business depends on the accuracy of your estimates. YOU CANNOT BE TOO CAREFUL!

Neither the Frank R. Walker Co., the editor, the author nor the sources listed in the back of this book guarantees or warrants the correctness or sufficiency of the information contained in this book; nor do any parties assume any responsibility or liability in connection with the use of this book or of any products, processes or pricing described in this book.

FRANK R. WALKER COMPANY

PREFACE

It has been a long time since this country has seen an industry come of age as fast as the insulation industry. In fact it has come about so fast, that few people in the industry recognize their true (one could also add new) responsibility.

The current energy crisis will be with us through the decade of the '80's and could even extend into the '90's. Energy as we knew it in the '70's will never again be as abundant or as cheap. And, until new technology develops new energy sources, the responsibility for making our current energy supplies go further, rests as heavily on the insulation and construction industry as it does on the government, the utility industry and the auto industry.

Unfortunately, for people in the insulation industry, the decade is not going to be an easy one. Not since the pharmaceutical industry came under government scrutiny in early 1960 has another industry, in this case the insulation industry, been the center of so much legislative attention.

The greatest single problem in this decade will be the amount of legislation enacted by national, state and local government agencies. Not only are they concerned with how well an insulation product will perform, they are also looking at how it should be applied and how much to apply.

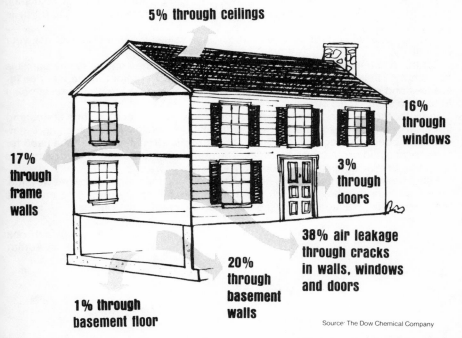

5% through ceilings

16% through windows

17% through frame walls

3% through doors

38% air leakage through cracks in walls, windows and doors

1% through basement floor

20% through basement walls

Source: The Dow Chemical Company

Insulation protection is needed in each of the major areas of heat loss. The figures are for a typical house with moderate insulation, insulated doors and double-glazed windows. The two-story structure has 2,000 square feet of opaque wall area with R-19 insulation in the ceiling, R-11 batts in the walls and one-half inch of fiberboard sheathing.

There is no question but what this will add a financial burden to the manufacturer and the applicator. But, it will have two positive effects.

First, it will drive out the marginal products and the unethical businesses. Second, it will clarify the gray areas in which manufacturers and applicators have heretofore been required to make judgemental decisions.

On the brighter side, a number of positive actions have taken place not the least of which are the tax credits offered by the Federal Government as an incentive to homeowners to reinsulate.

The credits apply to work done on the taxpayer's principal residence after April 19, 1977 and through 1985. In addition, low-income homeowners and renters can qualify for grants of up to $800 for materials and labor used to insulate ceilings, install storm windows, etc. For more information about these programs, contact your state energy office and ask about grants under the National Energy Act.

Under the National Energy Act of 1978, the Department of Energy is committed to reduce America's dependence on imported oil. To do this they developed the Residential Conservation Service Program (RCS). RCS is a state-run program that requires regulated utilities to offer certain services to the consumer. Non-regulated utilities not included in the state and the Tennessee Valley Authority must submit their own plans to DOE.

In summary, the utilities will supply customers with the following:
1. Energy audits that quote to the homeowner the cost and savings of each conservation measure; 2. A list of contractors who can do the work along with arrangements for financing and billing; 3. Follow-up inspection of the work.

Utilities are also involved in other ways, ranging from low-interest insulation loans to homeowners to home energy audits costing from $3.00 to $10.00 or in some cases even free.

And, if you are in doubt as to what the best R-values for your area are, ask your local utility.

On the one hand it would appear that for the insulating contractor the barrel is half empty. He is beset on all sides by consumers, government, material price increases and escalating labor rates. If he is going to survive the 1980's he is going to have to sharpen his business accumen.

In truth, though, the barrel is half full. Not only has the contractor's status and importance changed for the better, the insulation industry is approaching a new level of modern day technology. Today the public is strongly aware of the need for the services and products he provides. The stature of the insulating contractor has risen to a professional level unthought of even five years ago.

Many products manufacturers and contractors will falter and fall by the wayside. Those who survive, however, will find the decade financially rewarding and have the personal satisfaction of knowing they provide an essential service.

Harry Hardenbrook
Author

EDITOR'S NOTE

Although increases in energy costs showed some moderation in 1981–82, leading experts generally agree that they will rise faster than general inflation in the years to come. This will be particularly true for some of the high growth sun belt regions which will require the building of expensive new electrical power plants to meet demand. Also contributing to high energy costs is America's dependency on over 40 percent of its energy requirement from oil imports. Unfortunately, most of this comes from the highly volatile Middle-East.

Effective use of insulation in new and retrofit construction can be both cost effective for the consumer and profitable for the insulation contractor. However, reducing energy consumption through conservation benefits us in more ways than just saving money. These include: reducing our vulnerability to the whims of foreign powers controlling energy reserves, reducing pollution levels, reducing our balance of payments deficit, and improving the economic climate by reducing the inflation rate.

These and other reasons will create a need for skillful, technically competent insulation contractors for decades to come.

Gary D. Cook, Editor

TABLE OF CONTENTS

Chapter 1

FUNDAMENTAL CONCEPTS AND TECHNIQUES

To better understand the techniques of using and estimating insulation effectively, a conceptional understanding of heat transfer fundamentals is necessary. This chapter will address basic heat transfer theory and some of the terms used in the insulation trade. Other terms, definitions, and abbreviations are contained in the Glossary of Terms at the end of the book.

Heat.—Heat energy is the random motion of molecules in matter. The more violent this motion, the greater the temperature and potential for heat transfer to cooler objects. Heat always moves from warmer to cooler places. Temperature is the level of intensity of heat, while the quantity of heat is measured in British Thermal Units (BTU's).

One BTU is equal to the amount of heat necessary to raise one pound of water one degree Fahrenheit. This is approximated by burning a wooden kitchen match. To remove 12,000 BTU's per hour from a building, an air conditioner rated at one ton capacity is required. With respect to substances at different temperatures (different levels of heat), heat can flow from the hotter one to the cooler one in one or more of three different ways: conduction, convection, and radiation.

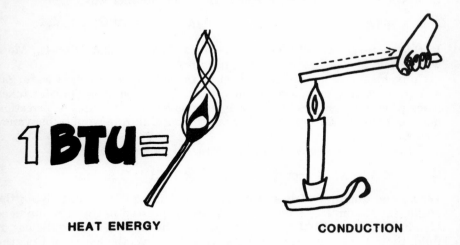

HEAT ENERGY
CONDUCTION

Conduction.—Conduction is the movement of heat through a material or from one material to another providing they are in contact with each other. Heat is transferred directly from molecule to adjacent molecule. Placing one end of a piece of pipe in an open flame will soon cause the other end to become hot due to conduction.

Four factors determine the amount of heat transferred by conduction through a building component (wall, ceiling, floor, etc.):

(1) the area (A), expressed in square feet (ft^2), of the building component separating the warm side from the cooler side,

(2) the overall coefficient of heat transmission or thermal transmittance (U-value), expressed in (BTU/hrft^2 °F), of the building component (obtained by adding the U-values or reciprocal of the thermal resistances (R-values) for each element in a section of the component),

(3) the temperature differential ($\triangle$T), expressed in (°F), between the environmental temperatures on either side of the building component,

(4) the length of time (t) in hours the heat transfer occurs under the prescribed conditions.

Simplified, heat transferred by conduction through a building component can be expressed by the formula:

$$Q = A \times U \times \triangle T \times t;$$

that is, the quantity of heat (Q) conducted through a material is equal to multiplying the area (A) times the thermal transmittance times the temperature differential ($\triangle$T) times the length of time (t). For sizing heating, ventilating, and air conditioning (HVAC) systems, the time is normally taken for the peak design conditions for one hour. For sizing HVAC equipment the formula can be reduced to:

$$Q = A \times U_t \times \triangle T \text{ (HVAC Sizing). Expressed another way:}$$

$$Q = A \times 1/R_t \times \triangle T \times t, \text{ or } Q = A \times 1/R_t \times \triangle T \text{ (HVAC Sizing).}$$

In this case, the overall thermal resistance is used so that $1/R_t = U_t$. More will be said about these relationships later.

Convection.—The transfer of heat by the actual movement of warm gas or liquid into cooler spaces is convection. Convective heat transfer takes place when air passing over a warm stove is heated and rises. Convection may be forced by fans or pumps or may be natural from wind or buoyancy forces.

Convective heat transfer can be expressed by the formula:

$$Q = h_a \times A \times \triangle T \times t, \text{ or } Q = h_a \times A \times \triangle T \text{ (HVAC Sizing).}$$

Where the quantity of heat transferred (Q) is equal to multiplying the coefficient of convective heat transfer (h_a), expressed in the same units as U-values (BTU/hrft^2 °F), times the area of the surface next to the gas or fluid, times the temperature differential ($\triangle$T) times the length of time the transfer takes place. The reciprocal of the coefficient of convective heat transfer (h_a) may be listed in some manuals as air film R-values and may be used as an R-value when computing the overall U-value across a building component section. The R-value for outside air film for winter conditions is generally taken for 15 mph wind and is 0.17 ft^2 hr °F/BTU. The air film R-value for summer conditions is taken for wind at 7½ mph and is 0.25 ft^2 hr °F/BTU.

Radiation.—The transfer of heat away from a relatively hot object across an open space or vacuum by means of electro-magnetic waves such

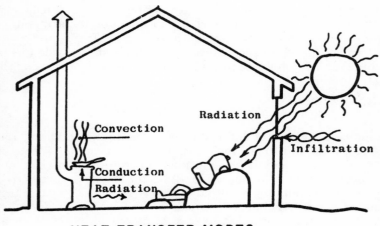

HEAT TRANSFER MODES

as infared rays is called radiation. All the heat received by the earth from the sun is transferred by radiation. It is the only form of heat transfer that can cross a vacuum. When people sit in front of a fire they feel mostly radiant heat. The rate in which radiant heat is transferred is proportional to the absolute temperatures raised to the fourth power. In the insulation trade, radiant heat is accounted for by using the standard conduction heat transfer formula and replacing the expression for temperature differential ($\triangle T$) with equivalent temperature differential ($\triangle T_e$) such that:

$$Q = A \times U_t \times \triangle T \times t, \text{ or } Q = A \times U_t \times \triangle T_e \text{ (HVAC Sizing)}.$$

The equivalent temperature differential ($\triangle T_e$) depends on a number of factors including the geographical location, orientation, time of day, month, and certain characteristics of the material receiving the radiation such as color and mass. These are listed in various air conditioning and heating manuals such as ASHRAE Fundamentals, Carrier System Design Manual, and Air Conditioning Contractors of America (ACCA) manuals.

Infiltration.—Infiltration may be classified as a special form of convection. Convection normally takes place in a defined envelope, whereas infiltration is an exchange of energy between the inside and outside of a building. Infiltration can cause a large amount of energy to be used in a home or building. This occurs when unconditioned outside air leaks inside through openings in the building envelope such as cracks around windows and doors, and openings that accommodate wiring, piping, and flues.

Calculating energy losses due to infiltration is as much an art as a science. Since losses can be considerable, contractors sizing HVAC equipment must consider infiltration accurately.

There are several factors influencing the quantity of heat transferred through infiltration:

(1) the volume of the air exchanged per unit time between the inside and outside is usually expressed in cubic feet per minute (CFM) or building

volume times the number of air changes per hour (V × AC/hr), (2) the heat capacity of the air which is dependent on its temperature and pressure is usually in the range of 0.018-0.022 BTU/ft^2 °F, and (3) the temperature difference between the inside and outside ($\triangle$T).

Thus the infiltration losses in BTU's/hr can be estimated using the appropriate formula below:

$$Q = CFM \times 1.2 \times \triangle T, \text{ or } Q = V \times AC/hr \times 0.02 \times \triangle T.$$

For example, calculate the infiltration heat losses in a building 150 feet long, 50 feet wide, and 10 feet high when the infiltration rate is equal to 1.5 air changes per hour and with the inside temperature maintained at 70°F and the average outside temperature 40° F for the hour considered. The volume (V) of the building equals 150 × 50 × 10 or 75,000 cubic feet and the temperature differential ($\triangle$T) equals 70°F − 40°F or 30°F. Substituting these values in the formula Q = V × AC/hr × 0.02 × $\triangle$T, the heat loss (Q) can be determined.
Q = 75,000 × 1.5 × 0.02 × 30 = 67,500 BTU/hr.

How may cubic feet per minute of infiltration occurs in this example? Taking the volume (V) of 75,000 ft^3 and multiplying it by 1.5 AC/hr the infiltration rate of 112,500 ft^3/hr is obtained. Dividing that by 60 minutes per hour, 1875 CFM of air is found to enter this building by infiltration. Substituting that value in the equation:

Q = CFM × 1.2 × $\triangle$T; Q = 1875 × 1.2 × 30 = 67,500 BTU/hr or the same answer as before.

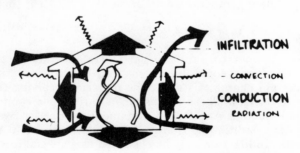

COMPARATIVE HEAT LOSS

Applying the Concepts.—Insulation contractors are primarily concerned with reducing energy losses in buildings that occur through the envelope. The appropriate formula for computing hourly energy losses (HVAC sizing) deserves further analysis:
Q = A × U × $\triangle$T (Generally used to calculate conductive winter heating loads with radiant heat gains usually neglected), or
Q = A × U × $\triangle$T$_e$ (Used to calculate summer cooling loads with solar radiant gains figured in).

Energy savings or conservation within the building envelope can be attacked in three ways:

(1) Reduce the building surface area (each component) by half and the heat transfer can be reduced by half. This can be done in the design stage by selecting a floor plan minimizing the wall and roof areas per conditioned floor area. A multistory cube shaped building will be more energy efficient than a single story rectangular building with the same floor area.

(2) Reduce the coefficient of heat transmission (U) by one half and heat transfer can be reduced by one half. This can be done by increasing the thermal resistance (R-value) by adding insulation in each component.

(3) Reduce the temperature differential by half and the heat transmission will be reduced by half. This can be done by adjusting the inside temperature (thermostat setting) closer to the outside ambient temperature. The temperature differential can be compared to voltage in electrical theory, the higher the $\triangle T$ the greater the potential for heat transfer.

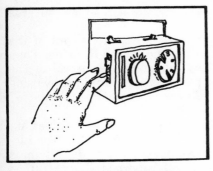

ADJUST THERMOSTAT

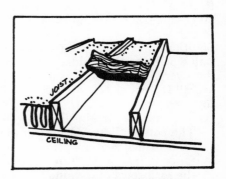

INSTALL INSULATION

From a practical standpoint, it is generally easier to affect changes in the (U) value by increasing insulation, rather than reducing the area or temperature differential. After the floor plan is selected, the area of the building envelope becomes fixed. There are comfort limitations to adjusting thermostat settings below 68° F in the winter and above 78° F in the summer. The insulation contractor can excel by selecting the proper type and amount of insulation. This can result in major energy cost savings for the owners or tenents of a building.

R-value and U-value Determinations.—Resistances (R), Conductances (C), or Conductivities (k) for various insulation materials and building materials are contained in the chapters that follow. There are also examples showing the overall thermal resistance (R_t) or transmittance (U_t) across a building component section. The following methodology, used for determining the overall U_t or R_t —values, will apply throughout this handbook.

For example the wall section illustrated by the accompanying figure is constructed as follows: (R_1) is ¾ " plywood exterior siding (k = 0.8), (R_2) is ½ " fiber board sheathing (C = 0.76), (R_3) is 3 ½ " fiber glass batt insulation between studs (C = 0.091), and (R_4) is painted ⅝ " gypsum board (R = 0.56). Also, the outside temperature is taken to be 30° F with the outside air film assumed for winter conditions (R_o = 0.17) and the inside temperature is maintained at 70°F with the air film assumed for still horizontal heat flow conditions (R_i = 0.68).

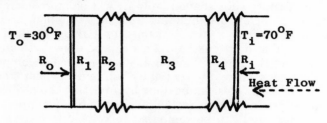

WALL SECTION EXAMPLE

Problem: (1) find the overall R-value of the wall section, (2) find the overall U-value, and (3) find the heat flow, in BTU/hr, through an 8' × 40' area of this wall.

Solution: first the R-values must be determined for each element of the wall which are then added together to arrive at the overall R_t-value. Then the overall U_t –values can be obtained by taking the reciprocal of the overall R_t –value (U_t = 1/R_t). Finally, the heat flow is determined by using the formula Q = A × U_t × $\triangle$T. These steps are illustrated as follows:

(1) The outside air film R_o was given as 0.17.

The conductivity (k) for plywood was given at 0.8. Since k-values are for 1" thick sections, this must be divided by 0.75 to get the conductance (C); C = 0.8/0.75 = 1.07. The resistance for R_1, by definition, is the reciprocal of C-value (R_1 = 1/C) or, for ¾" plywood, R_1 = 1/1.07 = 0.93.

The C-value for ½" fiber board sheathing was given as 0.76. Again R_2 = 1/C, substituting, R_2 = 1/0.76 = 1.32.

The C-value for 3½" fiber glass batt was given as 0.091. R_3 is the reciprocal of (C) or, R_3 = 1/0.091 = 11.

The R_4-value for gypsum board was given as 0.56.

Finally the inside air film R_i-value was given as 0.68.

Since all the heat flows across each element in the wall, the overall R_t-value for the wall section is solved using the same procedure as finding the overall resistance of a series of resistances in an electrical circuit: R_t = R_o +R_1 +R_2 +R_3 +R_4 +R_i = 0.17+0.93+1.32+11 +0.56+0.68 = 14.66 ft² hr °F/BTU. In this case, the fiber glass batt contributes to 75% of the total thermal resistance of the wall.

(2) Calculating the overall U_t-value of the wall section is easy from this point by using the expression:
U_t = 1/(R_o+R_1 +R_2 +R_3 +R_4 +R_i); or by definition, U_t = 1/R_t. Substituting the value for R_t calculated above; U_t = 1/14.66 = 0.068 BTU/ft² hr °F.

(3) Using the formula Q = A × U_t × $\triangle$T, the final part of the problem can be solved. The area (A) of the wall was stated as 8' × 40' or 320 ft². The U_t was calculated to be 0.068 BTU/ft² hr °F. The temperature differential ($\triangle$T) is obtained by subtracting the outside temperature from the

inside temperature (70–30) = 40°F. Substituting the appropriate values;
Q = 320 × 0.068 × 40 = <u>870</u> BTU/hr of heat is transferred through the wall under these conditions.

Estimating Energy Savings.—Frequently a contractor is asked to estimate the energy savings by adding insulation to a building component. Soaring energy costs have made this one of the more rewarding aspects of the trade.

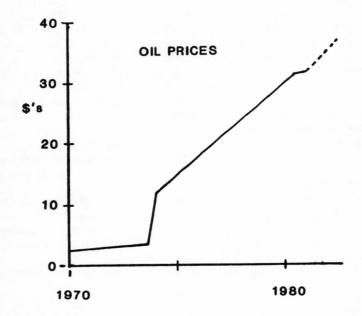

One method of estimating these savings is shown in the following example:

(1) In a New York locality listed as having 8000 heating degree days, estimate the winter heat savings in BTU by using ¾" polyisocyanurate foam sheathing rated R5.4 instead of the fiber board sheathing used in the previous example,

(2) estimate the energy cost saved if fuel oil (HV=140,000 BTU/gal) priced at $1.20/gal is used in a furnace that is 65% efficient, and how many years will it take to payback the extra investment if the foam sheathing costs $0.15/ft more, installed, than the mineral fiber, and

(3) estimate the savings if electric resistance heating is to be used and the cost of electricity is $0.08 per kilowatt hour (KWH) and how many years will it take to pay off the extra investment.

From the previous example the following values were given or determined: wall area (A = 320ft^2), outside air film (R$_o$=0.17), exterior plywood (R$_1$=0.93), fiber sheathing (R$_2$=1.32), fiberglass insulation (R$_3$=11), gypsum board (R$_4$=0.56), inside air film (R$_i$=0.68), and the overall R$_t$ −value was calculated to be <u>14.66.</u>

(1) Using the expression: $R_t = R_o + R_1 + R_2 + R_3 + R_4 + R_i$ and substituting 5.4 for R_2 (foam), the overall R-value for the modified wall becomes: $R_t = 0.17 + 0.93 + 5.4 + 11 + 0.56 + 0.68 = \underline{18.74}$

For determining seasonal heat transfer, the degree days multiplied by 24 hrs/day can be substituted for ($\triangle$T) in the formula:

$Q_1 = (A \times \triangle T)/R_t$ (remember $1/R_t$ can be substituted for U_t). The winter heat loss through the original wall can now be estimated:

$Q_1 = (A \times \triangle T)/R_t = 320 \times 8000 \times 24/14.66 = \underline{4,190,996}$ BTU/yr. The modified wall: $Q_2 = 320 \times 8000 \times 24/18.74 = \underline{3,278,549}$ BTU/yr. The winter savings now becomes $Q_s = Q_1 - Q_2$, or $\underline{912,447}$ BTU/yr.

(2) The cost of the fuel oil saved can now be estimated using the expression: E\$=$(Q_s \times Fc)/(HV \times Eff)$, with E\$=energy savings in \$/yr, Q_s =energy savings in BTU/yr (912,447), Fc=fuel cost in \$/unit (\$1.20/gal), HV=heating value of the fuel in BTU/unit (140,000 BTU/gal), and Eff=furnace efficiency (.65). Substituting, E\$ = $(912,447 \times 1.20)/(140,000 \times 0.65) = \underline{\$12.03/yr.}$ The foam sheathing cost 320×0.15 or \$48 more than the fiber. The simple payback can be estimated using the expression:

Payback=Investment/Savings= 48/12.03 = about $\underline{4}$ years.

The Department of Energy (DOE) considers a simple payback less than 6 years as being cost effective, so this modification should be recommended.

(3) The electricity cost saved can be estimated using the expression in (2) above: E\$=$(Q_s \times Fc)/(HV \times Eff)$, with Fc=\$0.08/KWH, HV for electricity = 3413 BTU/KWH, and the furnace efficiency for electric resistance heating is usually assumed as = 1.0. Substituting these values: E\$ = $(912,447 \times 0.08)/(3413 \times 1.0) = \underline{\$21.39/yr}$

To estimate the payback substitute the appropriate values in the expression:

Payback = Investment/Savings = 48/21.39 = $\underline{2.24}$ years (excellent payback). Of course, the annual savings can be even higher if air conditioning is used in the summer. This portion of the annual savings can be estimated similar to above using the cooling degree days $\times$ 24 for ($\triangle$T) instead of the heating degree days.

Proper Amount, Selection and Installation.—Too frequently, a building designed to certain insulation standards will not perform as expected after it is built. Investigations have shown the most likely cause to be either improper amount, selection, or installation of the insulation.

Amount.—There is a map in the Chapter titled Mineral Wool/Fiber Glass that provides the DOE recommended levels of insulation. The amount of insulation recommended may be based on this, but a more accurate estimation would be based on the cost verses savings (payback) analysis. Both winter heating and summer cooling requirements should be considered.

Selection.—There are tables in the back of this handbook that are designed to assist the contractor in selecting the proper insulation for a job. There are certain considerations that must be made in selecting the type of insulation for a particular application. For example, it is important that insulation selected for wall cavities will not shrink or settle with time. There have been many cases where the initial performance of the insulation has been excellent, but after a few years performance declined considerably. Ureaformaldehyde foams must be mixed with great accuracy, otherwise excess shrinkage and harmful unpleasant fumes can occur. If mixed properly these problems can be minimized.

Loose fill insulation, such as mineral wool and cellulose, may compact and settle after a period of time causing its effectiveness to decline. With the exception of certain closed-cell foam insulations, most insulations cease to be effective when they become wet. Proper installation of a vapor barrier usually minimizes this problem.

Installation.—The installation of insulation is a facet of the trade that requires close supervision. Gaps around wiring and electrical outlet boxes, piping runs, and next to framing members create heat short circuits and convective thermal drafts. This causes a disproportionate degradation of insulation performance. In fact, research has shown that gaps in insulation within wall cavities amounting to only three percent of the total area will degrade the actual performance up to twenty percent.

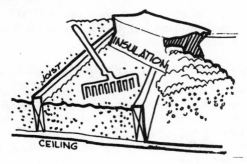

INSTALL PROPERLY

Sealing openings where wiring and piping runs transverse floors and ceilings through sole and top plates is very important. In residential construction up to twenty percent of infiltration heat losses occur by not attending to this problem. There are a variety of caulking and foam products suitable for this purpose.

Compressing insulation beyond the specified density drastically reduces the insulating value in most cases. For example, if a 5½" fiber glass batt rated at R19 is compressed to 3" it will perform at less than R10. Even if the correct quantity of insulation is blown or poured into an attic it will not give the R-value expected unless it is raked to the proper density and depth.

Chapter 2

BUILDING CODES

GOVERNMENT SPECIFICATIONS, TECHNICAL STANDARDS AND MODEL BUILDING CODES

In order to protect the contractor as well as the consumer, all insulation products must meet certain standards and pass certain tests as determined by the Government (i.e. the General Services Administration) and the ASTM (American Society For Testing and Materials).

Since these standards and tests are revised from time to time, it is important for the architect, builder, contractor, etc., to be aware of such revisions. When a new specification is issued, all previous specifications in that category are invalid. For a federal specification the final letter is important because it identifies the latest revision. Thus HH-I-1030 has been superseded by HH-I-1030A.

Current ASTM tests can be identified by the last two numbers which denote the year of issue. Thus, ASTM C687-71 was issued in 1971. If it is reapproved later this is indicated in parenthesis, while the letter "E" indicates an editorial change.

The following government specifications and ASTM tests cover insulation products. Detailed information on these specifications and tests can be found in most libraries.

GENERAL SERVICES ADMINISTRATION SPECIFICATIONS

HH-I-515D	Federal Specification - Insulation Thermal (Loose Fill for Pneumatic or Poured Application) Cellulosic or Wood Fiber
HH-I-521E	Federal Specification - Insulation Blankets, Thermal (Mineral Fiber for Ambient Temperatures)
HH-I-523	Insulation Block and Pipe Covering Thermal (Calcium Silicate, for Temperatures up to 1200°F)
HH-I-524B	Federal Specification - Insulation Board, Thermal (Polystyrene)
HH-I-525	Insulation Board, Thermal Cork
HH-I-526C	Federal Specification - Insulation Board, Thermal (Mineral Fiber)
HH-I-527	Insulation Board, Thermal (Building Board, High-Strength, Sheathing)
HH-I-529B	Federal Specification - Insulation Board, Thermal (Mineral Aggregate)
HH-I-530A	Federal Specification - Insulation Board, Thermal (Polyurethane or Polyisocyanurate)
HH-I-551E	Federal Specification - Insulation Block & Boards, Thermal (Cellular Glass)
HH-I-558	Insulation, Blocks, Boards Blankets, Felts, Sleeving (Pipe and Tube Covering), and Pipe Fitting Covering Thermal (Mineral Fiber, Industrial Type)

HH-I-561	Insulation Block and Sleeving, Thermal (Asbestos-for Temperatures up to 1200°F)
HH-I-574B	Federal Specification - Insulation, Thermal (Perlite)
HH-I-585C	Federal Specification - Insulation, Thermal (Vermiculite)
HH-I-1030A	Federal Specification - Insulation, Thermal (Mineral Fiber, for Pneumatic or Poured Application)
HH-I-1252B	Federal Specification - Insulation, Thermal, Reflective (Aluminum Foil)
HH-I-1972	Insulation Board, thermal faced, polyurethane or polyisocyanurate
LLL-I-535B	Federal Specification - Insulation, Board, Thermal (Cellulosic Fiber)

ASTM (AMERICAN SOCIETY FOR TESTING AND MATERIALS) TESTS

C167-64 (1976)	Standard Test Methods for Thickness & Density of Blanket or Batt Type Thermal Insulating Materials
C168-67	Standard Definition of Terms Relating to Thermal Insulating Materials
C177-76	Standard Test Method for Steady State Thermal Transmission Properties by Means of the Guarded Hot Plate
C236-66 (1971)	Standard Test Method for Thermal Conductance & Transmittance of Built-Up Sections by Means of the Guarded Hot Box
C303-77	Standard Test Method for Density of Pre-Formed Block-Type Thermal Insulation
C355-64 (1973)	Standard Test Methods for Water Vapor Transmission of Thick Materials
C518-76	Standard Test Method for Steady-State Thermal Transmission Properties by Means of the Heat Flow Meter
E84-79a	Standard Test Method for Surface Burning Characteristics of Building Materials

ASTM Tests can be conducted by competent independent laboratories using current ASTM methods.

Additional information covering insulation, vapor barriers, etc., can be found in the ASHRAE (American Society of Heating, Refrigeration and Air-Conditioning Engineers) Handbook, 1977 Edition, "Book of Fundamentals".

Model Building Codes.—There are three primary organizations in the United States which are non-governmental and have a great deal of influence on building materials and how they are used. In the case of each of these groups they have adopted working "Model" building codes which have been adapted, in lieu of writing their own, by many states, cities and municipalities. These "Model Building Codes" and the sections which apply to insulation are listed at the end of each chapter. Persons wishing more specific information regarding the codes may want to contact the organizations directly. They are:

SOUTHERN BUILDING CODE CONGRESS (SBCC)
900 Mt. Clair Rd. Birmingham, Alabama 35213
INTERNATIONAL CONFERENCE OF BUILDING OFFICIALS
(ICBO) 5630 S. Workman Mill Rd. Whittier, California 90601
BUILDING OFFICIALS AND CODE ADMINISTRATORS (BOCA)
17926 S. Halsted St. Homewood, Illinois 60430

Classification of Materials.—Depending upon the model building code used, insulation materials are classified as follows:

Class 1 -Flame spread 0-25
Class 2 -Flame spread 26-75
Class 3 -Flame spread 76-200

The Model Building Codes contain significant restrictions on the use of foam plastic insulation for building construction applications. The three codes are essentially equivalent in the following requirements:

1. No use of exposed foam plastic insulation in any interior application. (ICBO allowed limited use in agricultural buildings in the 1975 code but eliminated this exception in the 1976 code.)

2. All foam plastics shall have a flame spread rating* of not more than 75* and shall have a smoke developed rating of not more than 450 when tested by ASTM E-84, in the thickness and density intended for use. Exception is made to the smoke requirement for foam over 20 pounds per cubic foot, less than 1/2 inch in thickness, and covering not more than 10% of any wall or ceiling.

3. The room-side surface of foam plastic insulation must be fully protected from the interior of the building by a thermal barrier having a finish rating of not less than 15 minutes when tested by ASTM E-119, or qualify under Item 5 or 6 below. Thermal barriers shall be installed in a manner that they will remain in place for a minimum of 15 minutes under the same test conditions.

4. Foam plastics may be used in a roof covering if the foam plastic is a part of a Class A, B, or C roofing assembly. That plastic foam which is nearest the interior of the building shall be protected by an approved barrier. Other approved roof coverings may be applied over foamed plastic provided the foam is separated from the interior of the building by 1/2 inch plywood with blocked joints or equivalent material. (Reference ICBO only).

5. Foam plastic insulation having a flame spread* of 25* or less may be used in or on walls in a thickness of not more than 4 inches when the foam plastic is covered by a thickness of not less than 0.032 inch aluminum or No. 26 gauge galvanized sheet steel and the insulated area is protected with automatic sprinklers. Such walls shall not be used where noncombustible or fire-resistive construction is required. The Model Code organizations' Research Committees have issued recommendations on products for use in noncombustible or fire-resistive construction based upon available BTU contribution in the construction.

---

*This numerical flame spread rating is not intended to reflect hazards presented by this or any other material under actual fire conditions. In addition, states, cities and areas may adopt their own codes.

6. Foam plastic used in doors without a fire-resistive rating shall have a flame spread* of 25* or less. Such doors shall be faced with No. 26 gauge sheet steel or 0.032 inch aluminum. Doors which have been tested and found in compliance with ASTM E-152 need only contain foam with 75* flame spread*.

7. Since the above requirements could be overly restrictive, the codes specifically provide for approval of exceptions based upon approved diversified fire tests simulating the actual end use. The exact testing required will vary with the application and occupancy.

8. BOCA specifies that the products of combustion of an acceptable foam plastic shall be no more toxic than the combustion products of wood.

Any state or municipality which has adopted the 1975 BOCA code may enforce the code in the normal manner.

Although the above is believed to be accurate, prior to using foam plastic in any building construction application, the regulatory agency having actual jurisdictional authority over the proposed location should be contacted for guidance and approval.

Model Energy Codes.—Many states have adopted model energy efficiency codes. These codes are designed to fill the void left when the Building Energy Performance Standards (BEPS) failed to be adopted, or to comply with the Energy Policy and Conservation Act (Public Law 94–163). Some codes follow the ASHRAE 90–75 standard for building energy efficiencies, others are more rigorous such as Florida's Model Energy Efficiency Code for Building Construction. Florida's code provides a statewide standard for energy efficiency in the thermal design and operation of all buildings, and allows builders to follow either prescriptive minimum standards, or performance standards which allow for more design flexibility.

Builders and contractors should check with their local building officials for information about any energy codes that apply in their area.

All codes will take one of two forms . . . a specification or a performance code. The former will specify the material; the latter how the product or system should perform.

Since nearly everyone who builds or remodels will be affected by one code or another, it is mandatory that you be totally aware of the codes in your area.

In smaller communities this can generally be done simply by contacting the local Building Commissioner. In larger communities and cities it may be the Building Department. In still other areas the responsibility is handled by the Engineering Department or a Research Committee. Regardless of who has the responsibility you must know your building codes because the penalties for not knowing them can be rather severe.

---

*This numerical flame spread rating is not intended to reflect hazards presented by this or any other material under actual fire conditions. In addition, states, cities and areas may adopt their own codes.

Chapter 3

CELLULAR PLASTICS/
EXPANDED POLYSTYRENE

CELLULAR PLASTICS

In the field of energy conservation, cellular plastics have carved an ever-growing niche as an accepted insulation material. Essentially there are four different products in this classification. Included are: expanded **polystyrene** (called EPS), **extruded polystyrene** (Dow Styrofoam), **polyurethane** and **polyisocyanurates.** They offer a great deal of versatility and can be used for residential and commercial/industrial construction, both new and retrofit in a wide variety of applications. Although their characteristics are similar, their physical properties, insulating properties and end-use applications vary considerably. Because of these variations, a careful evaluation of the application and end use for each product should be made before the product is applied.

MOLDED POLYSTYRENE (EPS)

Manufacturing Process.—The use of molded polystyrene as an insulating product was established in the mid-1950's. In the most commonly used manufacturing process, polystyrene resins are steam heated, expanding the resins to beads which are 1/8 to 1/4-inch in diameter. After curing, the expanded beads are placed in a mold and again steam heated. At this stage, final expansion takes place and the beads are fused into what is called a billet or bun. Each of the beads is now fused into a composite mass, but *not* interconnected. It is the dead air space in each of the beads tht gives EPS its high insulation properties. After allowing their properties to stabilize, the billets are ready for cutting or fabricating into individual boards. Each is precisely cut to a specific width and thickness.

Expanded polystyrene is cut to specific widths and thicknesses with hot wires.

EPS is commonly used at a density of one pound per cubic foot. However, higher and lower densities are manufactured, and as energy costs escalate, higher density material is being specified. As a general rule, for most insulating applications, up to 2 lb. stocks are used and approved. Higher densities must be custom molded.

Principal Uses.—Depending upon the individual product, the primary uses for expanded polystyrene insulation include: commercial and industrial buildings in ceilings, roofs, walls, floors and foundations, and in controlled atmosphere applications. In residential construction, it is used for perimeter slab insulation, foundation insulation, exterior sheathing and siding backer-board. It is also being used in cathedral-type roof-ceiling applications.

R-Values.—Depending upon the ambient temperature, density and thickness of the board, expanded polystyrene will provide a wide range of R-values as indicated in the physical properties table below.

Physical Properties.—

Typical Physical Properties of EPS Board

Property		Units	ASTM Test	Density (pcf)		
				1.0	1.5	2.0
Thermal Conductivity	at 25F	BTU/(hr.)	C177 or	0.23	0.21	0.20
K Factor	at 40F	(sq. ft.) (F/in.)	C518	0.24	0.22	0.21
	at 75F			0.26	0.24	0.23
Thermal Resistance	at 25F	per inch		4.35	4.76	5.00
Values (R)	at 40F	thickness	—	4.17	4.55	4.76
	at 75F			3.85	4.17	4.35
Strength Properties						
Compressive 10% deformation		psi	D1621	13-17	21-27	30-38
Flexural		psi	C203	28-35	40-60	60-90
Tensile		psi	D1623	16-20	18-22	23-27
Shear		psi	D732	18-22	26-32	33-37
Shear Modulus		psi	—	280-320	460-500	600-640
Modulus of Elasticity		psi	—	180-220	320-360	460-500
Moisture Resistance						
WVT		perm-in.	C355	1.2-3.0	0.8-1.7	0.6-1.2
Absorption (vol.)		%	C272	less than 2.5	less than 2.0	less than 1.0
Capillarity		—	—	none	none	none
Coefficient of Thermal Expansion		in./(in.)(F)	D696	0.000035	0.000035	0.000035
Maximum Use Temperatures						
Continuous exposure		F	—	167	167	167
Intermittent exposure		F	—	180	180	180

Fire Resistance.—There are two grades or types of EPS available, depending upon the manufacturer. These are "modified" or "regular". Modified EPS contains a flame retardant additive which inhibits its burning characteristics under specified laboratory tests. Only "modified" grades of EPS are approved for all construction applications. The best guide is to purchase from manufacturers who are UL listed. NOTE: Since all EPS products are organic materials they must be considered combustible. They should not be exposed to ignition sources during shipment, storage, installation and use. USE ONLY AS DIRECTED ACCORDING TO THE MANUFACTURER'S SPECIFICATIONS.

Water Permeability and Moisture Absorption.—As the physical properties chart indicates, water vapor permeability is in the range of 1.2 to 3.0 perm-in. (ASTM-C355). Depending on density, water absorption is less than two per cent by weight (ASTM-C272).

APPLICATIONS

EPS should not be applied using solvent-based materials or adhesives, or finished with solvent-based paints. Do not leave exposed to sunlight. For additional information on product applications, consult the manufacturer or product literature.

FOUNDATION WALL APPLICATIONS

Perimeter Insulation.—When used as recommended, EPS qualifies for slab-on-grade perimeter insulation under HUD Materials Release #23la. To meet current HUD Minimum Property Standards,

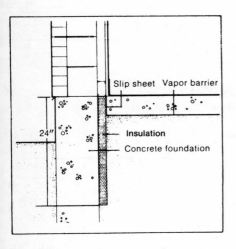

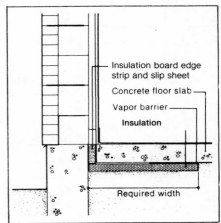

the following thicknesses of 24" wide EPS are recommended:

Unheated Slabs

Winter Degree Days	EPS Thickness
4000 or less	1"
4001 to 8000	1½"
8001 or more	2"

Heated Slabs

Winter Degree Days	EPS Thickness
2000 or less	1"
2001 to 3000	1¼"
3001 to 5000	1½"
5001 to 8000	2"
8001 or more	2½"

SIZES. Available in 12", 16" and 24" widths, standard 8'0" length, thicknesses and densities may be ordered to meet specific heat transmission and coefficient loading requirements.

To comply with FHA moisture protection requirements, use a vapor barrier rated at one perm or less when tested in accordance with ASTME-154 or ASTME-96. The material cost per bd. ft. of EPS for the above averages: 1" thickness $0.16; 1-1/4" $0.20; 1-1/2" $0.24; 2" $0.32; and 2-1/2" $0.40. For vapor barriers see Page 97.

AVERAGE EPS COSTS PER SQ. FT.
(TRUCKLOAD) 0-300 MILES

⅜" White Board	$ .045/sq.'	1" White Board	.107/sq.'
⅜" x 4' x 8'	1.44/sheet	1" x 4' x 8'	3.42/sheet
⅜" x 4' x 9'	1.62/sheet	1" x 4' x 9'	3.85/sheet
½" White Board	.061/sq.'	1 ¼" White Board	.132/sq.'
½" x 4' x 8'	1.95/sheet	1 ¼" x 4' x 8'	4.22/sheet
½" x 4' x 9'	2.20/sheet	1 ¼" x 4' x 9'	4.75/sheet
⅝" White Board	.071/sq.'	1 ½" White Board	.159/sq.'
⅝" x 4' x 8'	2.27/sheet	1 ½" x 4' x 8'	5.09/sheet
⅝" x 4' x 9'	2.56/sheet	1 ½" x 4' x 9'	5.72/sheet
¾" White Board	.083/sq.'	1 ¾" White Board	.181/sq.'
¾" x 4' x 8'	2.66/sheet	1 ¾" x 4' x 8'	5.79/sheet
¾" x 4' x 9'	2.99/sheet	1 ¾" x 4' x 9'	6.52/sheet
⅞" White Board	.097/sq.'	2" White Board	.204/sq.'
⅞" x 4' x 8'	3.10/sheet	2" x 4' x 8'	6.53/sheet
⅞" x 4' x 9'	3.49/sheet	2" x 4' x 9'	7.34/sheet

FOIL FACED SHEATHING
(TRUCKLOAD) 0-300 MILES

¾" Foil Faced	$ .203/sq.'	1 ½" Foil Faced	.267/sq.'
¾" x 4' x 8'	6.50/sheet	1 ½" x 4' x 8'	8.54/sheet
¾" x 4' x 9'	7.30/sheet	1 ½" x 4' x 9'	9.61/sheet
1" Foil Faced	.215/sq.'	1 ¾" Foil Faced	.288/sq.'
1" x 4' x 8'	6.88/sheet	1 ¾" x 4' x 8'	9.22/sheet
1" x 4' x 9'	7.74/sheet	1 ¾" x 4' x 9'	10.37/sheet
1 ¼" Foil Faced	.24/sq.'	2" Foil Faced	.312/sq.'
1 ¼" x 4' x 8'	7.68/sheet	2" x 4' x 9'	9.98/sheet
1 ¼" x 4' x 9'	8.64/sheet	2" x 4' x 9'	11.23/sheet

Buying from a lumber yard in less than truck load quantities, add 20-25% to the listed prices.

Labor Costs To Place Perimeter Insulation.—In most cases, since no attachment other than back-fill is required, a man should be able to place approximately 3200 sq. ft. of expanded polystyrene board stock per 8-hour day, at the following labor cost per 100 sq. ft.:

	Hours	Rate	Total	Rate	Total
Carpenter	.25	$	$	$13.35	$3.34
Cost per sq. ft.		....	....		$0.03

Crawl Space.—For this application, EPS can be mortar, adhesive or mechanically applied. Building codes require an approved thermal barrier (such as 1/2" gypsum board) having a finish rating of 15 minutes or more when tested according to ASTM Standard E-119. To meet HUD Minimum Property Standards, the following thicknesses of EPS are recommended for walls of heated crawl spaces and basements.

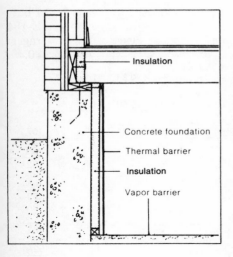

One and Two Family Construction

Winter Degree Days	Insulation Thickness
2501 to 4500	1½"
4501 and over	2½"

Multi-Family Construction

Winter Degree Days	Insulation Thickness
2501 to 4500	1"
4501 to 6000	1½"
6001 and over	2"

To meet FHA moisture protection standards, a maximum 1.0 perm vapor barrier must be provided on foundation wall and ground. The cost per bd. ft. of EPS for the above use averages: 1" thickness $0.16; 1-1/4" $0.20; 1-1/2" $0.24; 2" $0.32; and 2-1/2" $0.40. The average cost of 1/2" gypsum per sq. ft. is $0.16. For vapor barriers see Page 97.

Labor To Insulate Crawl Space.—A carpenter and mason should be able to place 400 sq. ft. of expanded polystyrene board stock and 1/2" gypsum board per 8-hour day, at the following labor cost per 100 sq. ft.:

	Hours	Rate	Total	Rate	Total
Carpenter	2	$....	$....	$13.35	$26.70
Mason	2	....	....	$13.12	$26.24
Cost per sq. ft.		....	....		$ 0.53

EXTERIOR WALL APPLICATIONS

Cavity Walls.—In cavity walls EPS can be laid-up dry using wall tie connections or appropriate spot applied adhesive. Under normal conditions a 1 lb. per cubic foot density of expanded polystyrene may be used without a vapor barrier, providing a 1/2" air space is left between the insulation and outer wall containing weep holes.

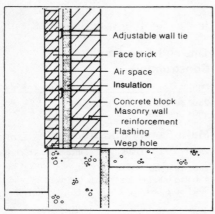

Adjustable wall tie
Face brick
Air space
Insulation
Concrete block
Masonry wall reinforcement
Flashing
Weep hole

Typical U Values   Cavity Wall

Wall Construction	No Insu-lation	1½"	2½"
		INSULATED	
4" Brick and 4" Concrete Block	0.34	.11	.08
4" Brick and 8" Concrete Block	0.30	.11	.07
4" Brick and 8" Cinder Block	0.25	.11	.07

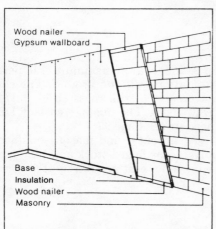

Wood nailer
Gypsum wallboard
Base
Insulation
Wood nailer
Masonry

Typical U Values   Drywall Base

Wall Construction	No Insu-lation	1"	2"	3"
		INSULATED		
8" Concrete Block	.41	.15	.09	.07
12" Concrete Block	.39	.15	.09	.07
8" L.W. Block	.35	.14	.09	.06
12" L.W. Block	.29	.12	.08	.06

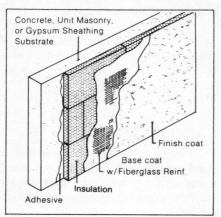

Concrete, Unit Masonry, or Gypsum Sheathing Substrate
Finish coat
Base coat w/Fiberglass Reinf.
Insulation
Adhesive

Typical "U" Values   Exterior Wall

Construction Type	1" Insulation	2" Insulation
Wood Stud	.14	.086
Metal Stud	.145	.088
4" Concrete	.18	.10
8" Concrete Block	.14	.093
8" Cinder Block	.14	.088

Labor To Insulate Cavity Walls.—A carpenter should be able to place 1600 sq. ft. of cavity wall per 8-hour day at the following labor costs per 100 sq. ft.:

	Hours	Rate	Total	Rate	Total
Carpenter	.5	$....	$....	$13.35	$6.68
Cost Per sq. ft		....	....		$0.07

Drywall Base.— EPS can be bonded directly to masonry walls with mortar or appropriate spot applied adhesives. Applied in this manner, EPS provides a self-furring solid backup for adhesive application of gypsum board. Supplementary attachment or vertical furring is strongly recommended to assure integrity of the gypsum board thermal barrier.

Labor Costs.—A carpenter and mason should be able to place 1600 sq. ft. of expanded polystyrene board stock and gypsum board per 8-hour day, at the following labor cost per 100 sq. ft.:

	Hours	Rate	Total	Rate	Total
Carpenter	.5	$....	$....	$13.35	$6.68
Mason	.5	....	....	$13.12	$6.56
Cost per sq. ft		....	....		$0.13

Exterior Walls.—Combination thermal insulation and exterior finish systems, suitable for new construction and retrofit are designed to minimize structural thermal stresses, eliminate cold spots on wall interiors, and reduce peak demands for heating and cooling in masonry construction. EPS board stock for the preceeding comes in 1" x 2' x 7' and 1" x 4' x 8' boards at an average cost of $0.16 per bd. ft. Gypsum board 1/2" x 4' x 8' costs approximately $5.00 per board. A carpenter should be able to place approximately 1600 sq. ft. of expanded polystyrene per 8-hour day at the following labor cost per 100 sq. ft.:

	Hours	Rate	Total	Rate	Total
Carpenter	.5	$....	$....	$13.35	$6.68
Mason	.5	....	....	$13.12	$6.56
Cost per sq. ft		....	....		$0.13

Exterior Sheathing.—Nonstructural EPS exterior sheathing used in connection with full stud cavity insulation, meets or exceeds current energy-saving standards, eliminating conversion to extra depth framing. Using full wall coverage and tight joints, EPS sheathing in place of conventional gypsum or wood fiber sheathing results in high thermal efficiency and reduced air infiltration losses. EPS sheathing products are available in sizes suitable for economical, efficient vertical application; butt or TG edging; with or without reflective foil membranes. They are manufactured to the requirements of HUD Use of Materials Bulletin #71. Designed solely for use with corner bracing (1" x 4" let-in or equivalent) to provide racking resistance, nonstructural EPS exterior sheathing is not intended for nail base applications. Moderate permeability to moisture vapor provides desirable cold-side breathing and condensation control when used in combination with a warm-side vapor barrier.

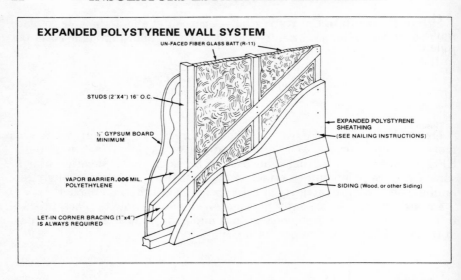

Reflective faced sheathing is designed for vertical installation over exterior sides of studs. It is installed in the same manner as conventional sheathing. Since it is nonstructural, an FHA let-in or diagonal bracing (with steel strap) is required. The 4-foot panel width allows for joints to meet at studs. Both faced and unfaced EPS can be applied using either 7/16" head roofing nails 4" on center or 3/4" crown staples 8" on center. Fasteners should be 2" or at least 1" longer than the thickness of the EPS. A carpenter should be able to place 1600 sq. ft. of expanded polystyrene per 8-hour day at the following labor cost per 100 bd. ft.:

	Hours	Rate	Total	Rate	Total
Carpenter	.5	$	$	$13.35	$6.68
Cost per bd. ft		. . . .	. . . .		$0.07

Masonry Fill.—Granulated EPS is also used as a pourable, free-flowing masonry fill insulation in concrete block cores or masonry wall cavities. Although the fill is inherently water resistant, normal design considerations covering wind-driven moisture should be followed. In addition to granulated EPS, special inserts are also molded for use in the cores of concrete blocks. Such applications supplement the thermal resistance of lightweight insulating blocks, enabling such systems to economically meet Local, State and Federal design requirements.

Installation

Insulation is poured directly into the wall from the bag or from a hopper placed on top of the wall. Pours may be made at any convenient interval, but the height of any pour shall not exceed 2 feet. Light rodding or tamping is necessary. Block joints at pilasters or other vertical members shall be mortared in by the mason to prevent leakage. Glass fiber rope or screen shall be used in weep holes to prevent leakage. During construction the insulation in the wall cavity should be protected from rain.

Granulated EPS comes in 4 and 10 cubic feet bags which cost approximately $4.00 to $5.00 and $7.50 to $8.50 respectively. A mason should be able to pour and fill approximately 800 sq. ft. of 12" block per 8-hour day at the following labor cost per 100 sq. ft.:

	Hours	Rate	Total	Rate	Total
Mason...	1	$ . . .	$ . . .	$13.12	$13.12
Cost per sq. ft..............................		. . .	. . .		$ 0.13

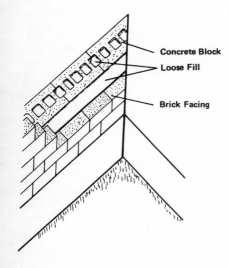

Concrete Block

Loose Fill

Brick Facing

Typical U Values—Cavity Walls

Wall Construction	No Insulation	Cavity Insulated
4" Brick/4" Block	0.34	0.10
4" Brick/6" Block	0.27	0.10
4" Brick/8" Block	0.25	0.09

Note: Values based on 2-cavity block and 3" wall cavity.

Typical U Values—Unit Masonry Walls

Block Type	No Insulation	Insulated
6" Lightweight	0.37	0.18
8" Lightweight	0.34	0.13
8" Sand/Gravel	0.52	0.33
12" Lightweight	0.29	0.09
12" Sand/Gravel	0.50	0.22

Note: Values based on 2-cavity block; calculations include allowance for radiation and convection factors.

APPROXIMATE COVERAGE
4-cubic-foot bags required to fill.

Sq. ft. of wall area	1" Cavity	2" Cavity	2½" Cavity	4½" Cavity	8" Block	12" Block
100	2	4	5	9	7	13
500	10	20	25	45	34	63
1,000	21	42	50	95	69	125
2,000	42	84	100	189	138	250
3,000	62	124	150	279	207	375
5,000	104	208	250	468	345	625
7,000	146	292	350	657	483	875
10,000	208	416	500	950	690	1250

100 bags per 8-hour day

Model Building Codes.—Expanded polystyrene must meet the following: Hud Bulletin (MB-74) paragraph 6.2.10; Uniform Building Code (ICBO)Section-1717; Basic Code (BOCA) Section-876.5; and Standard Building Code (SBCC) Section-717.

Manufacturers.—Among the leading suppliers of EPS board stock are the following: Drew International, Monticello, AR. 71655; W. R. Grace & Co., Cambridge, MA. 02140; Holland Industries, Inc., Gilman, IA. 50106; Southeastern Foam Products, Conyers, GA. 30207; and Western Insulfoam Corp., Kent, WASH. 98031.

Chapter 4

CELLULAR PLASTICS/
MOLDED POLYSTYRENE

EXTRUDED POLYSTYRENE (Dow Styrofoam*)

Manufacturing Process.—Unlike expanded polystyrene (EPS) which is molded, Styrofoam brand insulation is extruded, utilizing a somewhat different manufacturing process. Styrofoam is manufactured by flowing a heated mixture of polymers through a shaped opening to form a continuous board. Gases within the material cause it to expand as it leaves the opening. The result is a fine, closed-cell structure somewhat more resistant to water than molded polystyrene, urethane, fibrous glass, or loose materials. Whereas EPS is a generic product, manufactured by a number of companies, Styrofoam is a proprietary product manufactured only by Dow Chemical Company.

Except for special applications, Styrofoam is manufactured in several standard configurations. Styrofoam SM is an extruded board, blue in color, with butt edges, used extensively in wall and foundation insulation. Styrofoam TG is also extruded and blue. It has a high density skin with tongue and groove edges which additionally help control air infiltration.

For most insulating applications, stock averaging 40 psi compressive strengths are used and approved. Higher compressive strengths can be special ordered where required.

Principal Uses.—Styrofoam insulation is designed for use in commercial and residential construction, both new and retrofit. It may also be used in roofing, foundation and sub-soil applications, farm buildings, low temperature warehouses and food processing plants.

---

* a registered trademark of The Dow Chemical Company

All photos and illustrations this chapter courtesy Dow Chemical U.S.A.

Remodeling contractors can install a complete package of exterior home improvements as part of a single energy efficient project, including retrofit application. Extruded polystyrene board-form insulation is nailed directly over the home's existing exterior sidewall finish as part of a standard residing job.

R-Values.—R-values of standard products are shown below:

Thickness of Styrofoam SM and TG Brand Insulations and Average "R" Value

Thickness	"R" Value at 40°F Mean Temperature	"R" Value at 75°F Mean Temperature
¾"	4.1	3.8
1"	5.4	5.0
1½"	8.1	7.5
2"	10.8	10.0

Physical Properties.—

Average Properties of STYROFOAM Brand Insulation[1]

Property Description	ASTM Test	SM/TG	IB	RM
Insulation Properties Thermal Conductivity "k" (BTU/hr°F Sq. Ft./In.)	C-177-76-76E[2] and/or			
5-yr. Aged (Design) Values[3]	C-518-76E[2]			
@ 75°F Mean		.20	.25	.20
@ 40°F Mean		.185	.23	.185
Fresh (As Manufactured Value) at 40°F Mean[4]		.11	.16	.11
5 yr. Aged "R" Value For 1" Material (Aged Values) (°F Sq. Ft./BTU)				
@ 75°F Mean		5.0	4.0	5.0
@ 40°F Mean		5.4	4.3	5.4
Water Resistant Properties				
Water Absorption—Test Precision ± 1% (% by volume)	D2842-69	1	1	1
Water Vapor Permeability (Perm-Inch)	C355-64	.6	.9	.4
Physical Properties				
Compressive Strength[5] (lb./Sq. Inch)	D-1621-73	40	40	45
Min. (Design) Value		25	25	25

(1) The properties of STYROFOAM brand insulation are average figures obtained by ASTM test procedures where applicable. For property ranges or specification limits consult a Dow representative.

(2) See current test method for editorial comment. There are still serious problems to be solved before full implementation of ASTM Methods C177-76 and C518-76 will be practical. Traditional methods are therefore still being used by the industry to determine the thermal resistance of thick, low density insulations. The uncertainty in values is believed to be less than 10% for thick STYROFOAM insulations but an appropriate safety factor is recommended in systems where this may be critical.

(3) Based on five year aging of one inch samples at 75°F.

(4) Fresh or "as manufactured" k factors are presented for comparative purposes only. Dow recommends that the aged or longterm values be used as a design guideline.

(5) Compressive strength at 0.1" deformation. For structural applications involving continuous high compressive load, non-uniform loads, or high temperature, provide an adequate safety factor, or design-stress levels to minimize deformation with time.

Fire Resistance.—Styrofoam contains a flame retardant additive to inhibit accidental ignition from small fire sources. During shipping, storage, installation and use it should not be exposed to flame or other ignition sources. Styrofoam is combustible and constitutes a fire hazard if improperly used or installed. It should be adequately protected and used only as directed according to the manufacturer. It has a flame spread rating of less than 25. This rating is not intended to reflect the performance of this material under actual fire conditions.

Water Permeability and Moisture Absorption.—Styrofoam is a uniform, closed cell structure with no voids between cells. As such, it is inherently resistant to all forms of moisture. There is no capillary action. It has a perm rating of .4 to .9. Water absorption is 1% as shown by ASTM-C2842-69.

APPLICATIONS

Prolonged exposure to sunlight will cause discoloration and dusting of the surface which will impair the adhesive or finish bond. This can be prevented by covering with a light colored or white opaque covering in outdoor storage. Should dusting occur it should be brushed off before applying and care taken to minimize worker exposure to the dust. Solvent-based materials, such as adhesives, wood preservatives or paints may attack the foam; consult the manufacturer or the manufacturer's sales literature.

Sizes and Costs

Available Sizes
Standard Production Sizes[1]

Product	Width & Length	Thickness (Inches)
SM	16" x 96"	1", 1-½", 2"
	24" x 96"	¾", 1", 1-½", 2"
	48" x 96"	¾", 1", 1-½", 2"
TG	24" x 96"	¾", 1", 1-½", 2"
	48" x 96"	¾", 1", 1-½", 2"

[1]Other sizes available on special request

Average Material Cost Per Sq. Ft.

Product	Thickness	Average Cost Per Sq. Ft.
SM	¾"	$.19
	1"	.25
	1-½"	.38
	2"	.50
TG	¾"	$.19
	1"	.25
	1-½"	.38
	2"	.50

Labor To Apply Exterior Sheathing.—Styrofoam brand insulation may be installed either horizontally or vertically to minimize application time and scrap loss. Both vertical and horizontal tongue and groove joints may occur anywhere; but, butt joints should occur over framing. Snug fits should be made at all foam joints and around projections through the foam to minimize air leakage. Small pieces may be used if they span the studs.

Extruded polystyrene insulation is attached to the frame of a home using staples or nails. Tongue-and-groove edges interlock to assure tight seal. Applied roofline to frostline, the insulation covers and insulates both the wood frame and the masonry foundation—two critical areas of heat loss that are usually ignored.

For fastening, ⅜" head nails or ¾" crown staples are recommended. 8" horizontal spacing along plates, sills, headers, etc. 12" vertical spacing along studs, criples, corner posts etc. For 7/6" crown staples, the spacing can be shortened to 6" horizontally and 8" vertically. Fasteners used on the finish siding can be credited toward the preceeding.

A carpenter and assistant should be able to place 2400 to 4800 sq. ft. per 8-hour day at the following labor cost per 100 sq. ft.:

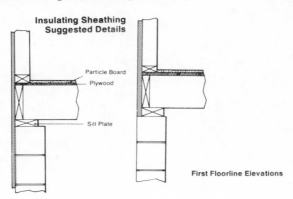

**Insulating Sheathing
Suggested Details**

Particle Board

Plywood

Sill Plate

First Floorline Elevations

	Hours	Rate	Total	Rate	Total
Carpenter	.22	$	$	$13.35	$2.94
Assistant	.22	. . . .	. . . .	$10.60	$2.33
Cost per sq. ft		. . . .	. . . .		$0.05

Labor To Insulate Exterior Walls Below Grade.—The primary method for insulating exterior basement walls is shown below, and on the next page.

A good foundation insulation system can cut home heat loss significantly.

THE PRIMARY METHOD

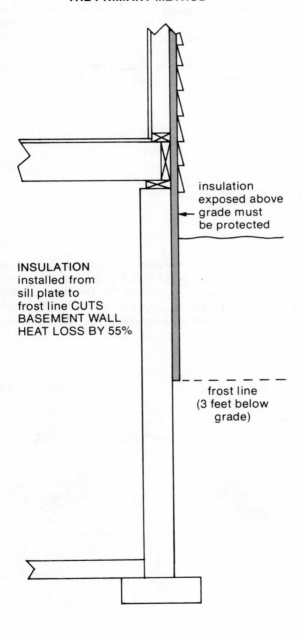

insulation
exposed above
← grade must
be protected

INSULATION
installed from
sill plate to
frost line CUTS
BASEMENT WALL
HEAT LOSS BY 55%

frost line
(3 feet below
grade)

In this method, coverage is continuous from the sill plate to the frostline. The exposed insulation above grade must be protected. The insulation is nailed into the box sill and nailed or glued to the above grade portion of the bare block or concrete wall. Below grade it is held temporarily by mastic spots and permanently by backfill.

A carpenter and assistant should be able to place 2000 to 4000 sq. ft. per 8-hour day at the following labor costs per 100 sq. ft.:

	Hours	Rate	Total	Rate	Total
Carpenter	.27	$....	$....	$13.35	$3.61
Assistant	.27	....	....	$10.60	$2.86
Cost per sq. ft.		....	....		$0.06

Labor To Insulate Slab-On-Grade.—Unheated slab-on-grade needs to be insulated only around the perimeter by running the insulation down the exterior side of the foundation wall to the frostline. Heated slabs require additional edge insulation. A carpenter and assistant should be able to place 2000 to 4000 sq. ft. per 8-hour day at the following labor cost per 100 sq. ft.:

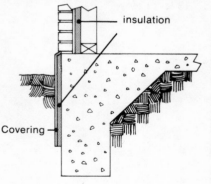

INTEGRALLY POURED SLAB-ON-GRADE

insulation

Covering

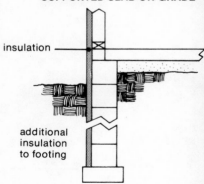

SUPPORTED SLAB-ON-GRADE

insulation

additional
insulation
to footing

	Hours	Rate	Total	Rate	Total
Carpenter	.27	$....	$....	$13.35	$3.61
Assistant	.27	....	....	$10.60	$2.86
Cost per sq. ft.		....	....		$0.06

Ceiling Applications. Labor To Insulate Sloped Ceilings.—As shown in the illustration below, the insulation is nailed to the underside of the rafters. Use a room side vapor barrier to protect the fiber batts. Vent the rafter cavity on the cold (exterior) side.

Sloped Ceiling

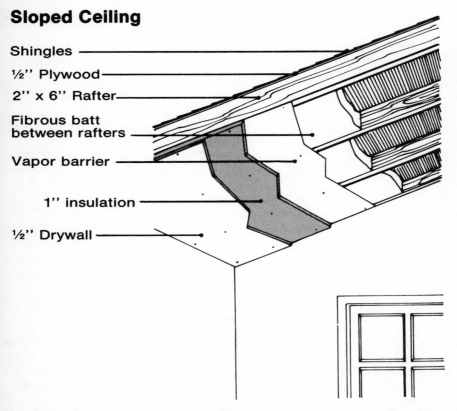

Shingles

½" Plywood

2" x 6" Rafter

Fibrous batt between rafters

Vapor barrier

1" insulation

½" Drywall

A carpenter and assistant should be able to apply 2000 to 4000 sq. ft. of insulation per 8-hour day at the following labor cost per 100 sq. ft.:

	Hours	Rate	Total	Rate	Total
Carpenter	.27	$	$	$13.35	$3.61
Assistant	.27	....	....	$10.60	$2.86
Cost per sq. ft.		....	....		$0.06

Model Building Codes.—Styrofoam brand insulation has been accepted by these government and model building codes as a nonstructural sheathing since 1969: BOCA No. 76-27; ICBO No. 2257; SBCC No. 7324; and HUD/FHA UMB-71.

Manufacturer.—The Dow Chemical Company, Midland, Michigan 48640.

Chapter 5

CELLULAR PLASTICS/UREA FORMALDEHYDE

UREA FORMALDEHYDE

Among the newer products which have gained increasing popularity as insulation materials are the foamed-in-place products typified by urea-formaldehyde. Initially it was developed in Europe for new construction and introduced into the United States in the late '60's. The first applications were in recreation vehicles and the OEM markets. Then, in the early 1970's, because it could be effectively applied to existing structures, it found its way into the residential retrofit market. In addition to its high R-value per inch, compared to other insulating products, urea-formaldehyde has the ability to completely fill regular and odd-shaped cavities containing pipes, wires, ducts, fixtures and other building elements.

On the other hand, these benefits have been offset by shrinkage and odor factors. A great deal of research has gone into eliminating both of these problems, and significant improvements have been made in the past two years, particularly the improvements in plasticizers to reduce shrinkage. Closer quality control in the blending of the chemicals has also been achieved by improved applicating equipment.

Unfortunately, desreputable installers or manufacturers have given Urea-formaldehyde a bad name due to improper formulation, mixing, or application. The Consumer Product Safety Commission (CPSC), after reviewing information on reported health problems due to formaldehyde fumes, has banned the use of urea-formaldehyde foam insulation (UFFI) in residences and schools, effective August 10, 1982.

The Consumer Product Safety Commission considers UFFI a hazardous consumer product because during and after the installation process, formaldehyde gas can be released and inhaled by the occupants. Inhaling formaldehyde vapors from UFFI has caused some persons to experience symptoms such as eye, nose, and throat irritation, persistent cough, respiratory distress, skin irritation, nausea, headaches, and dizziness. The severity of these illnesses varies from short-term discomfort to serious impairment. Of the occupants living in the more than 500,000 homes with UFFI insulation, only a very small percentage have reported health related problems.

The CPSC reports that although people vary in their susceptibility to formaldehyde, over 80 percent of healthy adults will experience no adverse reaction on levels less than 0.25 parts per million. Although the evidence is not conclusive, formaldehyde levels less than 0.1 parts per million are considered relatively safe for healthy adults.

In addition to UFFI, many other products give off formaldehyde fumes. Some of these may include carpets, draperies, and textiles having formaldehyde agents used in their dyeing process.

If unacceptable levels of formaldehyde fumes are determined to originate from UFFI, the insulation contractor may take or recommend certain steps to minimize the danger. Some of the steps, also recommended by the CPSC, include: 1) repairing all holes, cracks or gaps in the wall finish by caulking or spackling compounds; 2) sealing the walls with two coats of a vapor-barrier paint; 3) or installing mylar or vinyl wallpaper over the wall to reduce the flow of formaldehyde from the UFFI in the wall cavity. Special vinyl wallpaper paste and a good grade of canvas backed vinyl wallpaper should be used. Both the paint and the vinyl wallpaper will provide barriers reducing the penetration of moisture and fumes.

The CPSC ban applies to UFFI used in residences and schools. Use in commercial, industrial, and OEM markets have been exempted. If proper application and installation procedures are followed based on the products of reputable manufacturers, problems will be minimized and UFFI will meet appropriate building and test codes. If any doubt exists as to where it may be applied, it is recommended that the contractor either write or call: The office of the Secretary, Consumer Product Safety Commission, Washington, D.C. 20207; telephone (800) 638-2772 for continental U.S., (800) 492-8363 for Maryland only, and (800) 638-8333 for Alaska, Hawaii, Puerto Rico, and the Virgin Islands.

Manufacturing Process.—Urea-formaldehyde is generated at the application site as it is installed. It can be supplied fully diluted, partially diluted or in a dry-mix form. The foam, which looks much like shaving cream, is generated by combining an aqueous solution foaming agent con-

Illustrations this chapter courtesy Scientific Applications, Inc.

Urea-formaldehyde has been used in monumental construction such as Chicago's famous Water Tower Place.

taining a hardening agent and air. It is generated as it leaves the applicating gun. The mixing takes place in the gun where compressed air is mixed with the foaming agent to produce small bubbles which are expanded and coated with the urea-formaldehyde resin. As it leaves the gun, the foam contains about 75 percent water by weight. Curing starts immediately with initial set-up taking place in less than one minute. At this point, it can be troweled if necessary. Full cure time varies widely depending upon the manufacturer. Foam produced by this process contains approximately 60 percent closed and 40 percent open cells. Urea-formaldehyde has a shelf life which must be observed . . . three months for diluted material, up to two years for dry materials. Odor problems can occur from using a product which has passed its shelf life. A paint-like odor which may be noticed by some people is normal. It should disappear in one week to three months depending on temperature, humidity and ventilation.

Although urea-formaldehyde foams have been considered generic, the specific formulations used by different manufacturers are proprietary and include chemicals to improve their particular product. Also different types of applicating guns are used to produce the foam.

Principal Uses.—Urea-formaldehyde can be used for new as well as retrofit construction. Types of construction include residential, commercial/industrial and high-rise. Specific applications include block and block wall cavities, brick and brick cavities, retrofit brick and frame, concrete block, stud walls and precast hollow concrete.

R-Values.—R-values for urea-formaldehyde range from R-4.3 to R-4.9 per inch. However, the product can shrink while curing which will lower the installed R-value. Reported shrinkage rates vary from 1% to 6% and a rate greater than 6% should be considered faulty installation. To compensate for shrinkage, the U. S. Dept. of Housing and Urban Development developed a derating chart based on research by the U. S. Bureau of Standards. Using this chart, R-4.0 products with 6% shrinkage would be derated to R-2.8 per inch, and with 3% to R-3.4 per inch. Although manufacturers disagree with the HUD method, it is the only one available.

The table below shows the new R-values tested that will conform to F.T.C. regulations.

R-Values For Urea Formaldehyde
Tested @ 75°F.

Overall Thickness	R-Value
1"	4.38
2"	8.88
3"	13.29
3-½"	15.30

R-values will vary according to the product and the manufacturer. For specific R-values on a particular product, consult the manufacturer's literature or the manufacturer.

Physical Properties.—Typical physical properties, which can vary according to the manufacturer, are shown in the table below.

Physical Properties

Property		Value	Test Method
Thermal Conductivity:	at 25° F K factor	.206	ASTM C 177
	R factor	4.9	
	at 50° F K factor	.219	
	R factor	4.6	
	at 75° F K factor	.232	
	R factor	4.3	
(1) Density, standard, lbs./ft.^{3}			
Fresh weight, lbs./ft.^{3}		2.5-3.4	
(2) Linear Shrinkage, normal, percent		1.89	HUD/MB-74
Moisture Absorption			
	percent by volume	1.6	HUD/MB-74
Water Vapor Transmission, 24 hours in wet cavity wall,			
	perms	65	ASTM C 355
Calorific Value, BTU per Board Foot @ .7 lb./cu.ft.		393	ASTM D 2015
(3) Surface Burning Characteristics			
	(foam exposed) 3" E-84-77		ASTM E-84-77
Flame spread		15	
Smoke Density		15	
Fuel Contributed		0	

(1) Density can be varied from 0.6 to 1.0 lbs./ft.^{3}
(2) This shrinkage standard is based upon laboratory tests only, which do not represent actual conditions which may occur in the home.
(3) This numerical flame spread rating is not intended to reflect hazards presented by this or any other material under actual fire conditions.

Fire Resistance.—Fire behavior of urea-formaldehyde, like R-values, will vary according to the product and the manufacturer. In order to be acceptable, urea-formaldehyde should not exceed the following fire resistant standards as established by ASTM #E-84-77 with foam exposed:

Flame spread.. 75
Smoke developed... 450 in thickness of
intended use

On interior building surfaces, building codes require an approved thermal barrier (such as ½" gypsum board) having a finish rating of 15 minutes or more when tested according to ASTM Standard E-119.

Water Permeability and Moisture Absorption.—Moisture absorption for urea-formaldehyde will range from 1.6 to 2.0% by volume. Moisture content should comply with "HUD Use of Materials Bulletin-74". Water vapor transmission will range from 38 perms to 65 perms (using ASTM C355).

APPLICATIONS

A trained contractor and/or applicator are required for proper installation. Both should be trained and licensed by the material manufacturer in application procedures, and be able to show a certificate or identification card indicating that this training has been received. Installation should also be made in strict accordance with the manufacturer's operation procedures using only manufacturer's approved application equipment.

There are also temperature variables which should be observed. These include ambient temperatures at the time of installation; and temperatures of the materials being insulated. Particular care should be observed when the materials are being applied in areas where there are warm air conduits, light fixtures, heat vents, etc.

Material Prices.—Urea-formaldehyde is sold to insulating contractors or applicators in 55 gallon drums in wet form and 66 lbs. in two bags in dry form. The dry form is mixed with water in a drum at the application site. The cost per drum for both will range from $175.00 to $250.00 depending on the manufacturer. A drum will cover approximately 3,000–4,000 board ft.

Labor To Place Urea-Formaldehyde. Block and Brick Cavities, (new construction).

Courtesy Atamian Insulation, Barrington, Ill.

An experienced two-man crew should be able to install 4,000–6,000 board feet per 8-hour day at the following labor cost per 100 bd. ft.:

	Hours	Rate	Total	Rate	Total
Applicator	.16	$	$	$13.35	$2.14
Assistant	.16	....	....	$10.60	$1.70
Cost per bd. ft		....	....		$0.04

Brick and Brick Cavity (new construction).—An experienced two-man crew should be able to install 3,500–4,000 bd. ft. per 8-hour day at the following labor cost per 100 bd. ft.:

	Hours	Rate	Total	Rate	Total
Applicator	.21	$	$	$13.35	$2.80
Assistant	.21	....	....	$10.60	$2.23
Cost per bd. ft		....	....		$0.05

Retrofit Brick.—Small holes are drilled between the bricks and the foam is pumped in through a small nozzle. Bricks can also be removed to allow easier access to the cavity. An experienced two-man crew - including preparatory work and closing installation holes - should be able to install 2500–3000 bd. ft. per day at the following cost per 100 bd. ft.:

	Hours	Rate	Total	Rate	Total
Applicator	.29	$	$	$13.35	$3.87
Assistant	.29	....	....	$10.60	$3.07
Cost per bd. ft		....	....		$0.07

Concrete Block 12" (new and retrofit construction).—In new construction, the foam is inserted from the top when the block reaches a height of 6' to 8'. In existing block, the block is drilled and the foam is inserted into the core from the outside. An experienced two-man crew - including preparatory work and closing holes - should be able to install up to 4000–6000 bd. ft. per 8-hour day at the following cost per 100 bd. ft.:

	Hours	Rate	Total	Rate	Total
Applicator	.16	$	$	$13.35	$2.14
Assistant	.16	. . . .	. . . .	$10.60	$1.70
Cost per bd. ft.		. . . .	. . . .		$0.04

New Construction, Stud Walls.—In new construction, the foam is usually troweled in, in two applications. The cavity is slightly over-filled and then trimmed. The wall is immediately ready for interior finish. A vapor barrier should be applied to the warm side where required. A thermal barrier, such as ½" gypsum board, having a finish rating of 15 minutes or more should be applied over the vapor barrier. (See Page 12 for labor and material costs). An experienced two-man crew should be able to install 6000–8000 bd. ft. per 8-hour day at the following labor cost per 100 bd. ft.:

	Hours	Rate	Total	Rate	Total
Applicator	.11	$	$	$13.35	$1.47
Assistant	.11	. . . .	. . . .	$10.60	$1.17
Cost per bd. ft.		. . . .	. . . .		$0.03

Precast Hollow-Core Concrete.—An experienced two-man crew should be able to install 3000-4000 bd. ft. per 8-hour day at the following labor cost per 100 bd. ft.:

	Hours	Rate	Total	Rate	Total
Applicator	.23	$	$	$13.35	$3.07
Assistant	.23	....	....	$10.60	$2.44
Cost per bd. ft.		....	....		$0.06

Model Building Codes.—Urea-formaldehyde should meet the following: HUD Bulletin (MB-74) paragraph 6.2.10; Uniform Building Code (ICBO) Section-1717; Basic Code (BOCA) Section-876.5 and Standard Building Code (SBCC) Section-717.

Manufacturers.—The following are manufacturers of urea-formaldehyde with national distribution: Aerolite Division, Florence, KY.; Brekke Enterprises, Tacoma, WASH.; Celcius C.P. Chemicals, White Plains, N.Y. 10606; Rapco Inc., N.Y., N.Y. 10017 and Scientific Applications, Inc., Mt. Pleasant, IA. 52641.

Chapter 6

CELLULAR PLASTICS/ URETHANE AND ISOCYANURATE

URETHANE AND ISOCYANURATE

Manufacturing Process.—In cellular plastic insulation, urethanes and isocyanurates are among the newer entries. Both are manufactured through complex chemical reactions, and both can be manufactured by different processes. Simply stated, chemicals are mixed and metered onto a continuously moving conveyor, producing a continuous foam slab having essentially 90% closed cells; which is cut to specific lengths depending on ultimate end use. Both urethane and isocyanurates have a higher density at 2.0 lb. per cubic ft. than most EPS types at 1.0 lb. per cubic ft. Laminates are made by a similar process in which the mixture is metered between facer sheets. Urethane can be manufactured in both flexible and rigid form. For insulation, only the rigid form is used.

Foamed-in-place products are prepared by mixing or metering the chemicals and dispensing them either manually or automatically. Spray-on products utilize specially designed equipment for on-site application.

Principal Uses.—Both products are primarily used on new commercial/industrial buildings for roof insulation, floor and foundation insulation, cavity wall insulation, and in exterior/interior spray-on insulation. In residential construction, the principal use for isocyanurates is sheathing in new construction. However, depending on the particular product, it can also be used for exterior foundation insulation and slab-on-grade.

R-Values.—In the case of urethanes and isocyanurates, the blowing agents used in their manufacture is what gives them their excellent R-value. Consequently, the R-value per inch can range from a low of R-5.75 to a high of R-9.7. However, over a period of time these R-values can drop as air replaces the blowing agent. After the R-value stabilizes, it can be maintained with aluminum foil facing at least 1 mil thick and other laminates such as gypsum. Many manufacturers will show two R-values, "initial" and "aged".

Physical Properties—

Polyurethane/Polyisocyanurate Foams

Material Property	Value	Test Method
Density	2.0 lb/ft^3	
Closed Cell Content	90%	ASTM C591-69
Thermal Conductivity (k factor)	0.16–0.17 Btu-in/ft^{2}hr°F (aged & unfaced or spray applied) 0.13.0.14 Btu-in/ft^{2}hr°F (impermeable skin faced)	ASTM C177, C518
Thermal Resistance (R value) per 1" of thickness at 75F	6.2–5.8 hft^{2}F/Btu (aged unfaced or spray applied) 7.7–7.1 hft^{2}F/Btu (impermeable skin faced)	
Water Vapor Permeability	2 to 3 perm-in	
Water Absorption	Negligible	
Capillarity	none	
Fire Resistance	combustible	ASTM E136
Flame Spread	30–50 polyurethane 25 polyisocyanurate	
Fuel Contributed	10–25 polyurethane 5 polyisocyanurate	ASTM E84
Smoke Developed	155–500 polyurethane 55–200 polyisocyanurate	
Toxicity	produces CO when burned	
Effect of Age a) Dimensional Stability b) Thermal Performance	0-12% change 0.11 new 0.17 aged 300 days	ASTM D-2126
c) Fire Resistance	none	
Degradation Due To Temperature Cycling Animal Moisture Fungal/Bacterial Weathering	above 250°F not known none limited imformation available does not promote growth none	
Corrosiveness	none	
Odor	none	

Fire Resistance.—Since they are plastic materials, both urethanes and isocyanurates are combustible and must be covered with an approved thermal barrier (½") gypsum board or the equivalent having a finish rating of not less than 15 minutes) when used for most applications of thermal insulation. Isocyanurates, however, have a greater degree of heat stability and lower flammability characteristics than urethanes. Consequently, some isocyanurates have been approved for exposed use in certain commercial/industrial buildings. Typical burning characteristics for urethanes are a flame spread of 30–50*, a fuel contributed value of 10–25 and smoke developed from 155 to over 500. For foil faced isocyanurates, one manufacturer's product has a flame spread of 25 or less*; fuel contributed 5 to 15; and smoke developed 75 to 200. As in any insulation having flammability characteristics, each particular product must be weighed against its end

---

* The manufactures states that these numerical flame spread ratings are not intended to reflect hazards presented by these or any other materials under actual fire conditions.

use, and the manufacturer or manufacturers' literature carefully checked before the product is selected. As one manufacturer states: "We recommend that as a user of our material, you first check with your local building code officials and insurance agency personnel before application."

Water Permeability and Moisture Absorption.—Because of the high closed cell content, water absorption is negligible and vapor permeability is typically 2 to 3 perm-in for unfaced material. Foil-faced products also have negligible vapor permeability.

APPLICATIONS

When applying sprayed-on urethane, the time of the year and the temperature of the surface to be sprayed are important. Cold weather produces a lower yield. . . three board feet per pound in winter compared to four board feet in summer. Also there is considerable preparatory work; masking for example, to contain overspray. Application also requires fairly technical equipment, plus related back-up machines. Application should be made only by highly-skilled, thoroughly trained applicators.

URETHANE (Spray On)

Residential Construction.—Urethanes should be applied only by highly trained and fully qualified applicators. Consideration must be given to the design of the residence and the climatic environment in which it is being built before application. Since it is an organic material it must be protected from potential fire risks such as exposure to open flame or excessive heat. A thermal barrier must be applied which has a finish rating of 15 minutes such as ½" gypsum board or the equivalent. It must not be left exposed under any circumstances.

Cover Urethane Insulation with an Approved 15-Minute Finish Rated Thermal Barrier

Prior to installing urethane insulation, code officials should be consulted for recommendations and approvals. It is recommended that the thermal barrier be applied the same day the foam is installed.

All "hot" work should be completed prior to commencing installation. *Smoking in the area must be strictly prohibited.*

Preparatory Work.—All electrical boxes and connections such as for TV should be masked. Cover windows with polyfilm or other protective material. Seal windows and door framing, as well as holes for plumbing and

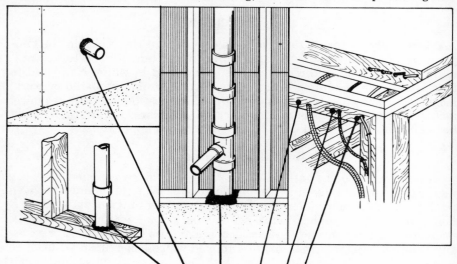

Polyurethane Caulking or Urethane Insulation

Courtesy The Upjohn Company

electrical wiring. Electrical wiring applications require specific attention and it is advisable to consult the foam manufacturer or the foam manufacturers' literature.

Urethane should not be applied under any circumstances in connection with aluminum wiring. The use of a vapor barrier on both sides of the insulation is recommended under certain conditions. Check with local authorities for standard area procedures.

Sizes and Costs. Materials.—Spray-on urethane is supplied in 55 gallon drums, weighing 10 lbs. per gallon depending on density. Density will also affect the coverage rate. Materials required can be estimated by establishing the volume of insulation needed (sq. ft. x thickness = board ft.). By knowing the foam to be used and the time of the year it is to be used, the estimated yield can be calculated by dividing the board feet into the estimated yield per lb. This will give you the board feet per lb., then divide the board feet per lb. into the total square feet to be covered and this will give you the number of lbs. of raw material required. Since most formulations are selling in the $1.00 per lb. range, costs for material will range from approximately $0.33 per bd. ft. (Winter) to $0.25 per bd. ft. (Summer), plus tax.

Labor To Insulate Wood or Channel Stud Walls.—Applications require a two-man crew. The insulation depth will depend upon the R-value desired. Once the house has been framed and enclosed, urethane is spray applied between the studs. This is best done by using a picture framing technique such as recommended by Upjohn. The applicator surrounds the

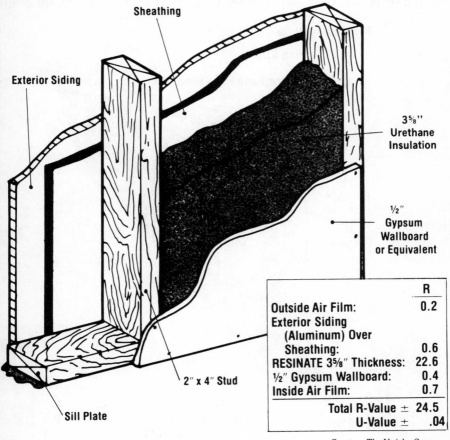

	R
Outside Air Film:	0.2
Exterior Siding (Aluminum) Over Sheathing:	0.6
RESINATE 3⅝" Thickness:	22.6
½" Gypsum Wallboard:	0.4
Inside Air Film:	0.7
Total R-Value ±	24.5
U-Value ±	.04

Courtesy The Upjohn Company

outside of the stud allowing the foam to rise along the stud face. After rising, the middle of the cavity is sprayed. This ensures sealing of cracks, and eliminates air-pockets and fold-over. Insulation depth can be checked by marking an ice pick in ½" increments and inserting it into the cured foam. Including preparatory work, a trained applicator and assistant should be able to spray 6000 to 7000 bd. ft. per 8-hour day at the following labor cost per 100 bd. ft.:

	Hours	Rate	Total	Rate	Total
Applicator	.12	$. . . .	$. . . .	$13.35	$1.60
Assistant	.12	. . . .	. . . .	$10.60	$1.27
Cost per bd. ft		. . . .	. . . .		$0.03

After installation, the walls must be covered with an approved 15 minute finish rated thermal barrier, such as ½" gypsum or the equivalent. (For cost of gypsum board application, see page 12).

Labor To Insulate Masonry Walls on the Interior.—Follow proper electrical and plumbing preparation procedures. Install 2" wood or metal furring strips, 24" on center. The resulting cavity is then filled by spray ap-

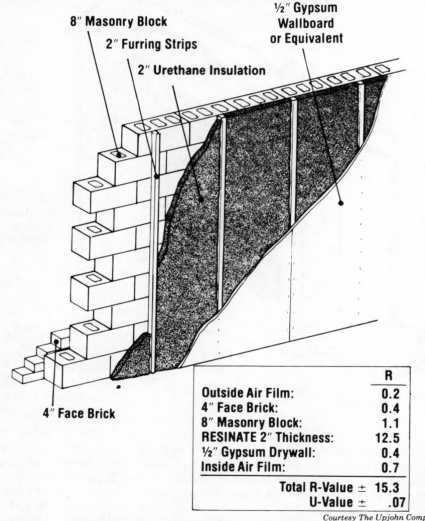

8″ Masonry Block
2″ Furring Strips
2″ Urethane Insulation
½″ Gypsum Wallboard or Equivalent
4″ Face Brick

	R
Outside Air Film:	0.2
4″ Face Brick:	0.4
8″ Masonry Block:	1.1
RESINATE 2″ Thickness:	12.5
½″ Gypsum Drywall:	0.4
Inside Air Film:	0.7
Total R-Value ±	15.3
U-Value ±	.07

Courtesy The Upjohn Company

plication. An applicator and assistant should be able to apply 6000 to 7000 bd. ft. per 8-hour day at the following cost per 100 bd. ft.:

	Hours	Rate	Total	Rate	Total
Applicator	.12	$. . . .	$. . . .	$13.35	$1.60
Assistant		. . . .	. . . .	$10.60	$1.27
Cost per bd. ft.		. . . .	. . . .		$0.03

Labor To Insulate Masonry Walls on the Exterior.—In this construction, urethane is applied to the exterior surface and then finished with stucco, masonry or similar finish. After spraying to the specified

Urethane Insulation to Design Thickness

8″ Masonry Block

Exterior Finish

Plasterer's Mesh

	R
Outside Air Film:	0.2
1″ Stucco:	0.2
RESINATE 2½″ Thickness:	15.6
8″ Masonry Block:	1.1
Interior Wall Finish (½″ Gypsum Drywall):	0.4
Inside Air Film:	0.7
Total R-Value ±	**18.2**
U-Value ±	**.05**

Courtsy The Upjohn Company

thickness, plasterer's mesh is installed and the desired finish applied. An applicator and assistant should be able to apply 7000 to 12,000 bd. ft. per 8-hour day at the following labor cost per 100 bd. ft.:

	Hours	Rate	Total	Rate	Total
Applicator	.08	$....	$....	$13.35	$1.07
Assistant	.08	....	....	$10.60	$0.85
Cost per bd. ft.		....	....		$0.02

Plaster's mesh or metal lath ranges in price from $0.20 to $0.27 per sq. ft.

FLOORS, FOUNDATIONS AND BASEMENTS

Labor To Insulate Foundation Exteriors.—In this application, urethane is spray-applied to the concrete block foundation to a depth of 3 inches, then covered with an asphaltic barrier for protection. The perime-

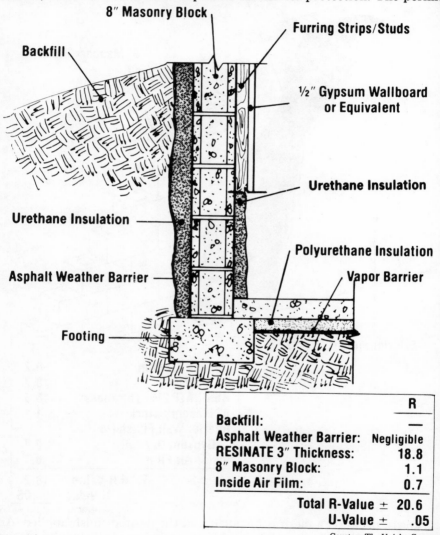

	R
Backfill:	—
Asphalt Weather Barrier:	Negligible
RESINATE 3″ Thickness:	18.8
8″ Masonry Block:	1.1
Inside Air Film:	0.7
Total R-Value ±	**20.6**
U-Value ±	**.05**

Courtesy The Upjohn Company

ter must be back-filled. An applicator and assistant can apply up to 12,000 bd. ft. per 8-hour day at the following labor cost per 100 bd. ft.:

	Hours	Rate	Total	Rate	Total
Applicator	.06	$. ...	$. ...	$13.35	$0.80
Assistant	.06	....	....	$10.60	$0.64
Cost per bd. ft.		....	....		$0.016

Labor To Insulate Inside Basement Sidewalls.—This application is used to form a seal against air infiltration from beneath the housing floor. Furring strips are installed as in interior walls and the resulting cavity filled with spray-applied foam. Proper preparatory procedures should be followed as specified by the manufacturer. The system must be covered with an approved 15 minute finish rated thermal barrier such as ½" gypsum board or the equivalent. An applicator and assistant should be able to apply 6000 to 7000 bd. ft. per 8-hour day at the following labor cost per 100 bd. ft.:

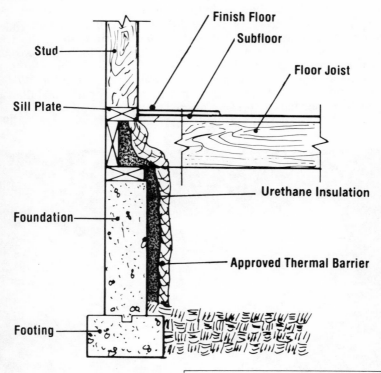

	R
8" Masonry Block:	1.1
RESINATE 1½" Thickness:	9.4
½" Gypsum Drywall:	0.4
Inside Air Film:	0.7
Total R-Value ±	11.6
U-Value ±	.09

Courtesy The Upjohn Company

	Hours	Rate	Total	Rate	Total
Applicator	.12	$. . . .	$. . . .	$13.35	$1.60
Assistant	.12	. . . .	. . . .	$10.60	$1.27
Cost per bd. ft.		. . . .	. . . .		$0.03

APPLICATIONS ISOCYANURATE AND URETHANE
(Board Stock)

Isocyanurate and urethane board stock can be used interchangeably in the following applications. However, since their physical properties vary somewhat, the product and its application should be carefully evaluated. It is also important to ascertain that the product meets local building codes and insurance regulations. Since these products have a closed cell structure, when they are foil faced they make an efficient barrier to moisture, as well as heat flow. Consequently, in colder climates there is the potential for trapped water vapor between studs to condense and accumulate in "porous cavity insulation materials", and cause a loss in insulation value. To provide assurance that moisture can escape, one manufacturer, the Celotex Corporation, recommends a Vent Strip System in certain areas of the country where winter degree days are 8000 or less. Based on climate, Celotex recommends the use of a vapor barrier/vent strip system as follows:

Area I: (4000 winter degree days or less) use: Properly installed 6 mil polyethylene vapor barrier on the interior side of the wall or foil back gypsum.

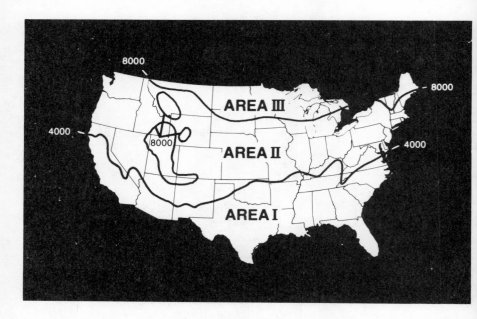

Area II: (above 4000 winter degree days) use: A properly installed 6 mil polyethylene vapor barrier on the interior side of the wall.

Area III: (8000 winter degree days or more). Celotex moisture vent strips should be used to supplement a properly installed 6 mil polyethylene vapor barrier.

As has been pointed out, urethanes and isocyanurates will experience a reduction in R-value after aging. This reduction will vary according to product, and aged R-values should be readily available from the manufacturer. Shown below is a typical set of R-values at the "time of manufacture and aged" as provided by the Celotex Corporation. The values shown are for standard width products.

Thermax "R" Values*—At Time Of Manufacture and Aged*

Nominal Thickness R Values	½"	⅝"	¾"	⅞"	1"	1¼"	1½"	1¾"	2"	2¼"
At Time of Manufacture 40° Mean Temp.	4.8	6	7	8.5	9.7	12	14.5	16.9	19	21.7
At 15 Months 40° Mean Temp.	4	5	6	7	8	10	12	14	16	18
At 32 Months 40° Mean Temp.	4	5	6	7	8	10	12	14	16	18
At Time of Manufacture 75° Mean Temp.	4.4	5.5	6.6	7.7	8.8	11	13.2	15.4	17.6	19.8
At 15 Months Aged 75° Mean Temp.	3.6	4.5	5.4	6.3	7.2	9	10.8	12.6	14.4	16.2
At 32 Months Aged 75° Mean Temp.	3.6	4.5	5.4	6.3	7.2	9	10.8	12.6	14.4	16.2

R values at time of manufacture are based on small scale K-matic tests. Aged R values are based on Guarded Hot Box Tests conducted in accordance with ASTM C236 on full sized product, and reported without air space effects.

Product Sizes and Costs.—Celotex Vent Strip is sold in ⅜" rolls of 100 ft. at an average cost of $0.04 per lineal ft. Standard board sizes (4'x8' and 4'x9') and average costs per board are shown in the table below:

	ISOCYANURATE		URETHANE (UTHANE 210®) For Commercial Application	
Size	Cost Per Sq. Ft.	Aged R-Value	Cost Per Sq. Ft.	Aged R-Value
½"	$0.235	4	$0.175	3.6
⅝"	.265	5	.22	4.5
¾"	.295	6	.26	5.4
⅞"	.335	7	.31	6.3
1"	.365	8	.35	7.1
1¼"	.425	10	.44	8.9
1½"	.495	12	.53	10.7
1¾"	.555	14	.61	12.5
2"	.615	16	.70	14.3
2¼"	.675	18	.79	16.1

Add 20% to the above for lumber yard delivery.

The following applications utilize foil-faced isocyanurate board stock, foil-faced on both sides. In most cases, unfaced urethane and isocyanurate can be applied in a similar manner. However, in some cases a separate vapor barrier may be required. To be safe, consult either the manufacturer or the manufacturer's literature before the product is applied.

Labor To Apply Exterior Sheathing.—Install acceptable corner bracing. If required, apply plastic vent strips fastened 12" o.c. to top plate only to vent wall moisture into attic. Install sheathing vertically with long joints in moderate contact, bearing directly on the framing members. Secure sheathing with galvanized roofing nails with ⅜" heads of sufficient length to penetrate framing a minimum of ¾", or use 16 gauge wire staples having a minimum of ¾" crown and leg length necessary to penetrate framing a minimum of ½". Care should be taken not to over-drive nails and penetrate facing. If staples are used, apply with crowns parallel to framing. Two men should be able to place 2400 sq. ft. per 8-hour day at the following labor cost per 100 sq. ft.:

	Hours	Rate	Total	Rate	Total
Carpenter	.33	$. . . .	$. . . .	$13.35	$4.41
Assistant	.33	. . . .	. . . .	$10.60	$3.50
Cost per sq. ft.		. . . .	. . . .		$0.08

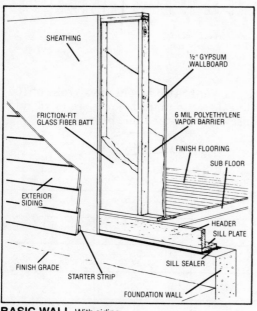

BASIC WALL With siding

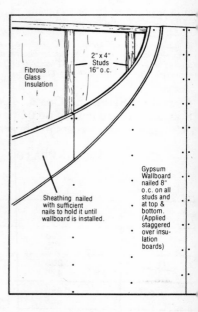

Courtesy The Celotex Corporati

Labor To Place Underlayment Frame Wall System.—This system requires sheathing, foil-faced on both sides, which, with taped joints and sealed penetration, serves as an effective vapor barrier. To maintain optimum vapor barrier protection, all sheathing joints and penetrations are taped with Celotex Aluminized Tape. The sheathing is applied to the interior stud surface and covered with ½" gypsum wallboard staggered over the sheathing joints. Two men should be able to place 2000 sq. ft. of sheathing per 8-hour day at the following labor cost per 100 sq. ft.:

	Hours	Rate	Total	Rate	Total
Carpenter	.4	$. . . .	$. . . .	$13.35	$5.34
Assistant	.4	. . . .	. . . .	$10.60	$4.24
Cost per sq. ft.		. . . .	. . . .		$0.10

MASONRY WALLS

Labor To Place Wood Furred System.—Wood furring may be fastened directly to the block or concrete and the sheathing applied to the furring;

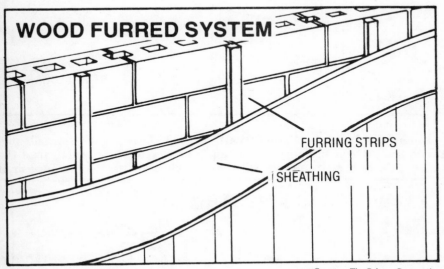

Courtesy The Celotex Corporation

or the sheathing may be spot adhered with construction adhesive directly to the block and wood furring applied over the insulation and secured to the block with masonry fasteners. Two men should be able to place 1000 sq. ft. per 8-hour day at the following labor costs per 100 sq. ft.:

	Hours	Rate	Total	Rate	Total
Carpenter	.8	$. . . .	$. . . .	$13.35	$10.68
Assistant	.8	. . . .	. . . .	$10.60	$ 8.48
Cost per sq. ft.		. . . .	. . . .		$ 0.19

Labor To Place Single Furred System.—Sheathing can be directly applied to the interior of the masonry wall, furring strips applied directly over the insulation and the wall finished with an acceptable interior finish. This system provides a thinner wall profile, while adding a single air space enhancing the thermal resistance. A carpenter should be able to install 500 to 600 sq. ft. per 8-hour day at the following labor costs per 100 sq. ft.:

	Hours	Rate	Total	Rate	Total
Carpenter	1.46	$. . . .	$. . . .	$13.35	$19.42
Cost per sq. ft.		. . . .	. . . .		$ 0.19

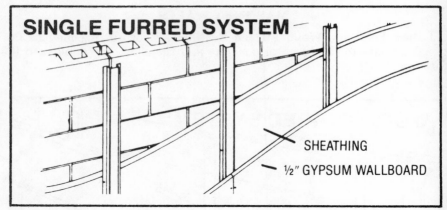

SHEATHING

½" GYPSUM WALLBOARD

Courtesy The Celotex Corporation

Labor To Insulate Cavity Wall.—Apply sheathing horizontally between the exterior masonry finish and the concrete block wall against the inner wall. Secure insulation with adjustable wall ties to masonry or if

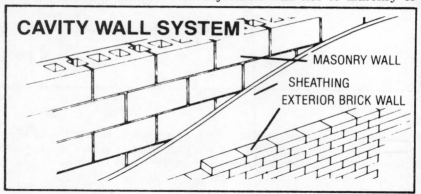

MASONRY WALL

SHEATHING
EXTERIOR BRICK WALL

Courtesy The Celotex Corporation

there are existing ties, impale sheathing on ties. A mason should be able to place approximately 80 sq. ft. per 8-hour day at the following labor cost per 100 sq. ft.:

	Hours	Rate	Total	Rate	Total
Mason	10	$....	$....	$13.12	$131.20
Cost per sq. ft.		....	....	$	$ 1.31

FOUNDATIONS

Labor To Place Interior Perimeter Insulation.—Lay a minimum 4 mil polyethylene vapor barrier over flat, smooth and dry well-tamped fill. Lay sheathing over the vapor barrier, staggering all joints and butt together. Pour concrete directly over sheathing. A carpenter should be able to place 9600 sq. ft. in an 8-hour day at the following labor costs per 100 sq. ft.:

	Hours	Rate	Total	Rate	Total
Carpenter	.08	$....	$....	$13.35	$1.07
Cost per sq. ft.		....	....		$0.01

Labor To Place Exterior Foundation Insulation.—In this system the insulation is continued into the ground on the exterior to the footings. Siding is applied in the normal manner. However, where mechanical back fill is used or the bottom edge of the siding is above ground level, provide suitable protection over the exposed or below grade insulation to avoid physical damage. All edges and joints should be taped. A carpenter should be able to apply 2400 sq. ft. in an 8-hour day at the following labor cost per 100 sq. ft.:

	Hours	Rate	Total	Rate	Total
Carpenter	.33	$. . . .	$. . . .	$13.35	$4.41
Cost per sq. ft.		. . . .	. . . .		$0.05

RETROFITTING

The following system is applied over existing siding and utilizes Celotex sheathing and venting strips. Before attempting to use another product for this system the manufacturer and the manufacturer's literature should be checked thoroughly to determine if the product is applicable.

The application which follows is a broad overview of how the system is applied. When using this system, applicators should contact the Building Products Division, Celotex Corporation for specific details.

Retrofitting using Celotex Retrovent Strips.

Old siding should be checked to be sure that it is in good condition, and repairs made as required. Evidence of existing moisture problems should be corrected. Celotex "Retrovent Strips", intended to provide vapor relief, should be applied as recommended, horizontally and vertically. Care should be taken not to block them off. The sheathing is applied vertically over the "Retrovent" strips. Attachment is by ⅜" diameter head galvanized nails or 1" crown 16 gauge staples with a minimum of ⅝" penetration into a nail holding substrate. At all wall and soffit junctures, the

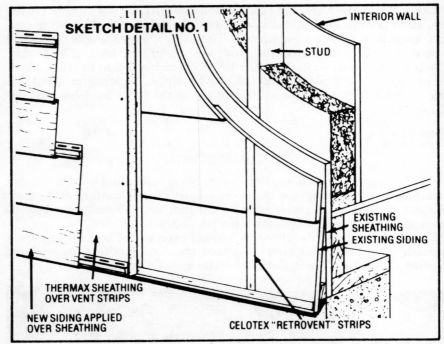

SKETCH DETAIL NO. 1

INTERIOR WALL

STUD

EXISTING SHEATHING
EXISTING SIDING

THERMAX SHEATHING OVER VENT STRIPS

NEW SIDING APPLIED OVER SHEATHING

CELOTEX "RETROVENT" STRIPS

Courtesy The Celotex Corporation

sheathing should be installed at least ¼ " below the soffit to provide an adequate moisture vapor relief exit.

Under windows and at walls below gables, specific installation procedures are required. New siding is applied generally in accordance with the manufacturer's instruction. Fasteners must be long enough to penetrate the sheathing into the substrate as recommended by the siding manufacturer. Two men should be able to prepare and apply 1200 sq. ft. of sheathing in an 8-hour day at the following labor rates for 100 sq. ft.:

	Hours	Rate	Total	Rate	Total
Carpenter	.66	$....	$....	$13.35	$8.81
Assistant	.66	....	....	$10.60	$7.00
Cost per sq. ft.		....	....		$0.16

Model Building Codes.—Urethane and isocyanurates must meet the following: HUD Bulletin (MB-74) paragraph 6.2.10; Uniform Building Code (ICBO) Section-1717; Basic Code (BOCA) Section 876.5 and Standard Building Code (SBCC) Section-717. Thermax TF 610 and 600 meet the following: ICBO 3223 (Technical Bulletin No. 1205); BOCA 77-36 (Technical Bulletin No. 1208); SBCC 7625-77 (Technical Bulletin No. 1206); HUD Materials Release 933a (Technical Bulletin No. 645).

Manufacturers.—Urethane and/or isocyanurate products are manufactured by the following companies: The Celotex Corporation, Building Products Division, Tampa, Florida, 33622; Rmax Inc., Dallas, Texas 75240; Panelera, Salt Lake City, Utah, 84104 and the Upjohn Company, Chemicals Plastic Research, Torrence, California, 90503.

Chapter 7

MINERAL WOOL/ROCK AND SLAG WOOL

MINERAL WOOL

Mineral wool, like cellular plastics, is a generic term which encompasses a number of different insulation materials. Included are rock wool and slag wool and fiber glass. In terms of usage they have been around longer than most other insulation materials in common use today. Even though there are newer products, mineral wools' popularity as an insulating material has not diminished. Although each products' characteristics are similar, like cellular plastics their physical properties and insulating values vary considerably. Therefore, particular attention should be paid to the manufacturer, the product and the product's end use before it is applied.

ROCK WOOL AND SLAG WOOL

Manufacturing Process.—The mineral wool industry began in the '20's. In the first manufacturing process, which is still in limited use today, molten rock or slag is passed in front of high speed steam jet. The molten stream is converted into drops by the steam. As the drops pass in front of the high velocity jet, fibers are formed by the streaming tails from the drops.

In the 1940's two other processes were developed. The first or Powell process utilizes a group of rotors operating at a fairly high R.P.M. The slag is deposited on the rotors as a thin film. As the rotors spin, the slag is spun off by centrifugal force forming the fibers.

In the second or Downey process the molten materials are fed onto a concave disk-shaped rotor. As the molten materials spin up over the disk edge they are fiberized by a high-speed steam or air jet.

The fibers are then bound together with a phenolic resin, compressed, and passed through a curing oven.

In each of the processes, the threads solidify into a wool-like mass, trapping many air pockets which gives mineral wool its insulation value.

Principal Uses.—Batts and blankets are designed to fit between framing members of residential and other light construction. Included are ceilings, attics, walls, floors, foundation walls and crawl space walls. Blown wool is generally applied to ceilings and sidewalls, unfloored attics, floored attics, attic knee walls and slopes and attic stairways.

WHERE TO INSULATE
A HOME

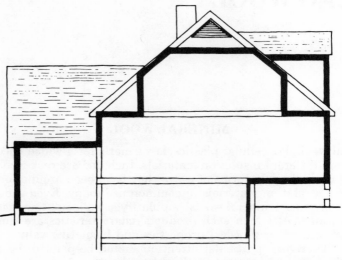

Illustrations this chapter courtesy Mineral Insulation Manufacturers' Association.

R-Values.—Mineral wool products are applied on the basis of their R-value. Care should be taken when installing batts or blankets not to compress them as this will reduce their R-value. The R-values for mineral wool will vary from R-2.1 to R-3.8 per inch. White wool has the highest R-value, while fiber glass has the lowest. Batts and blankets usually have higher R-values than blown-in or pourable material, with the exception of white wool. Blown products will have a lower R-value in an open space, such as an attic, and a higher R-value in a closed space, such as wall. Moisture will reduce its R-value. Therefore, it is common to install a vapor barrier on the warm side in winter.

APPROXIMATE R-VALUES BLANKETS

Thickness	Paper Faced	Foil Faced	R-Value
2	X	X	7
3	X	X	11
3-5/8	X		13
5-1/4	X	X	19
6	X	X	22

On faced batts and blankets, R-values are printed on the facing. Unfaced batts and blankets are coded with stripes or labels to identify the R-value.

Physical Properties.—

ROCK AND SLAG WOOL

Material Property	Value	Test Method
Density	**1.5-2.5 lbs/ft³**	
Thermal Conductivity	0.31–0.27 Btu-in/ft²hr°F (batts)	ASTM C177
(k factor) at 75F	0.34 Btu-in/ft²hr°F (loose fill)	
Thermal Resistance (R value)	3.2–3.7 hft²F/Btu (batts)	ASTM C177
per 1" of thickness at 75 F	2.9 hft²F/Btu (loose fill)	
Water Vapor Permeability	>100 perm-in	
Water Absorption	**2%** by weight	
Capillarity	none	
Fire Resistance	non-combustible	ASTM E136
Flame Spread	15	
Fuel Contributed	0	ASTM E84
Smoke Developed	0	
Toxicity	none	
Effect of Age		
a) Dimensional Stability	none (batt)	
	settling (loose-fill)	
b) Thermal Performance	none	
c) Fire Resistance	none	
Degradation Due To		
Temperature	none	
Cycling	none	
Animal	none	
Moisture	transient	
Fungal/Bacterial	does not support growth	
Weathering	none	
Corrosiveness	none	
Odor	none	

Fire Resistance.—The fibers of mineral wool are inorganic and are considered non-combustible. However, the facings on some batts and blankets are flammable. As soon as possible after installation, they should be covered with gypsum-board or other building code approved finish materials. Member companies of the Mineral Insulation Manufacturers Association state on all standard kraft paper and foil vapor barriers on batts and blankets "This vapor barrier is flammable and should not be left exposed." The material itself will not burn or melt at temperatures up to 1800°F.

Water Permeability and Moisture Absorption.—Mineral fibers are non-hygroscopic. Any moisture lies on the surface of the fibers, not inside them. Water vapor permeability is in the range of 100 perm-in. and water absorption up to 2% by weight.

Mineral wool will not trap moisture, causing condensation problems, but should be kept dry to retain its insulation value. Proper construction practices call for installing vapor barriers in walls of all new buildings. Local building practices and codes should be followed with regard to ceilings. When it is convenient, vapor barriers should also be installed in existing buildings.

APPLICATIONS
Rock and slag wool batts and blankets, and blowing wool

Rock wool and slag wool come in several different configurations. Batts and blankets with facings have flanges on left and right edges so that the insulation can be stapled to the studs to hold it in place. The facing can be either a vapor barrier or a "breather" paper. Vapor barrier facings are of aluminum foil (0.5 perm) or asphalt impregnated paper (1.0 perm, either black or brown in color). Only one face on a vapor-barrier faced product will be a vapor barrier. Any other paper facing on blankets or batts will be breather paper. Breather paper is installed to facilitate handling or provide flanges for stapling. Unfaced batts or blankets are designed to be held in place by pressure and supplement existing insulation.

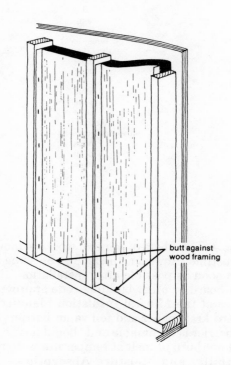

butt against
wood framing

Whenever mineral wool is installed, it should fit tightly on all sides. However, care should be taken not to compress the insulation as this will lower the R-value. If a batt or blanket is too long it should be shortened to fit, not folded over. If it is too short, cut a piece to fit the void. Batts and blankets with vapor barriers should be attached with the vapor barrier facing the warm side during the winter. Read the manufacturer's directions carefully to be sure all products are correctly installed.

Approximate Cost Per Sq. Ft. (Rock Wool)
Standard Sizes

R-Value/Thickness		Foil Faced	Paper Faced	Unfaced
R-11	3-½"	$0.18	$0.16	$0.15
R-13	3-⅝"			$0.21
R-19	6"	$0.29	$0.27	$0.26

Blankets come in rolls, with length depending on thickness and R-values. Standard widths are available for 12-, 16-, 20-and 24-inch o.c. wood framing; specified widths are available for steel studs. Batts are precut lengths of blanket, usually 48–96 inches long.

Labor Placing Ceilings.—When installing ceiling insulation at the same time as wall insulation, insulation is usually installed from underneath and held in place the same as with floors (see following). Batts and blankets, faced or unfaced, are installed between ceiling joists and butt-jointed at the ends. Faced batts should be stapled to joists. No stapling is required if insulation is laid in over finished ceiling.

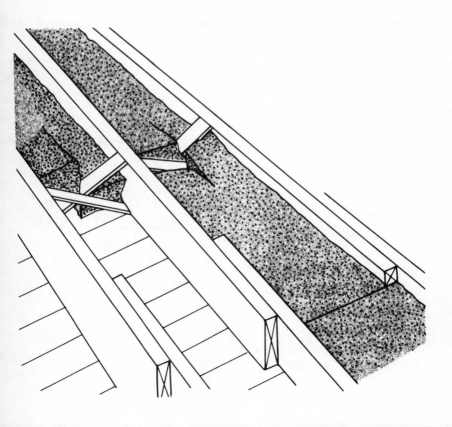

best attic insulation is obtained with first layer between joists and second at right angle layed across joists (this technique is not possible when pre-engineered trusses are used).

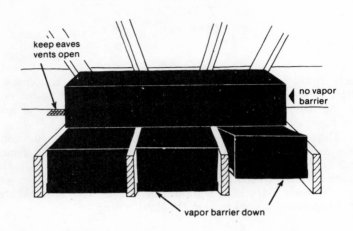

At least 1" clearance for air movement from soffit vent openings and ceiling grills *must* be maintained.

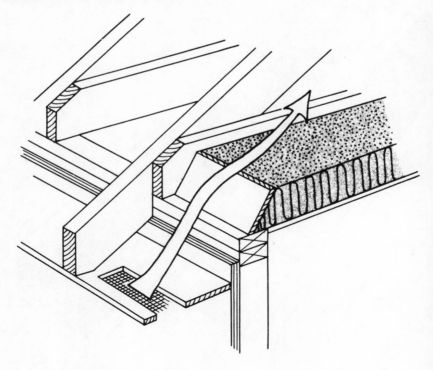

Insulation must be kept at least 3" from sides and 24" from the top of heat sources such as recessed light fixtures, ballasts, and HVAC equipment.

At least 1" air space for ventilation is recommended above all ceiling insulation.

Using R-19 batts, a carpenter should be able to insulate 1,700–2,200 sq. ft. of ceiling per 8-hour day at the following labor cost per 100 sq. ft.:

	Hours	Rate	Total	Rate	Total
Carpenter	.41	$....	$....	$13.35	$5.47
Cost per sq. ft.		....	....		$0.05

Attic Rooms.—Attics used as living space should be insulated as shown.

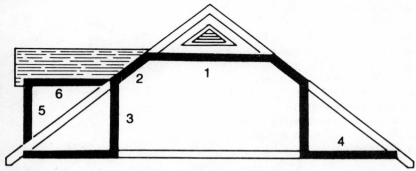

(1) Between collar beams. (2) Between rafters. (3) Knee walls. (4) Ceilings with cold space above. (5) Dormer walls. (6) Dormer ceilings.

Labor Placing Walls.— Fit insulation tightly to framing on all sides. Faced insulation can be stapled by "Inset" stapling or "Face" stapling.

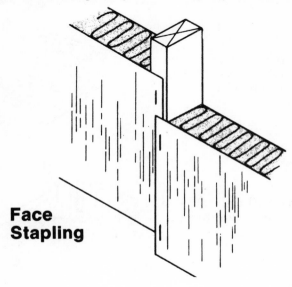

Face Stapling

Even the smallest opening between framing members should be insulated. A carpenter should be able to insulate 2500 sq. ft. of walls per 8-hour day at the following labor cost per 100 sq. ft:

	Hours	Rate	Total	Rate	Total
Carpenter	.32	$. . . .	$. . . .	$13.35	$4.27
Cost per sq. ft.		. . . .	. . . .		$0.04

Labor To Insulate Floors.— Install the material between floor joists. Vapor barriers should face the warm-in-winter side of the floor section. There are four methods of attachment:

1. *Wire fasteners.* This is the easiest and most effective method. The fasteners, preferably galvanized, are made for joist spacings of 12-, 16-, 20-and 24 inches. They can be used with metal, wood or concrete. The fasteners are placed by hand and bowed gently upward holding the insulation against the sub-flooring.

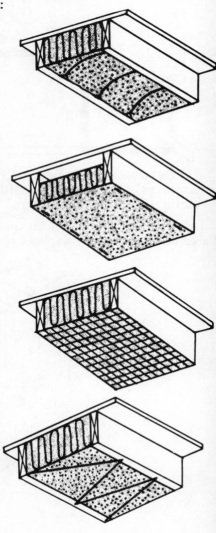

2. *Stapling.* Use reverse flange insulation which has a vapor barrier on one side and breather on the other with stapling flanges. The vapor barrier should face the warm-in-winter side.

3. *Mesh or screen.* After the insulation has been placed, staple wire or nylon screen to joist face.

4. *Wire Lacing.* Lace malleable wire by stapling or nailing to joist.

A carpenter should be able to apply 1700 sq. ft. of floor insulation per 8-hour day at the following labor costs per 100 sq. ft.:

	Hours	Rate	Total	Rate	Total
Carpenter	.147	$. . . .	$. . . .	$13.35	$6.27
Cost per sq.ft.		. . . .	. . . .		$0.06

Federal Specifications.— All mineral wool products should meet the following: Federal Specification HH-I-521E and HH-I-1030A.

APPLYING BLOWN ROCK WOOL

Blowing wool is specified by R-value and not inches of thickness. It must be installed so as to ensure proper density, coverage and minimum thickness. The best way to install the correct number of bags can be determined by the application table shown on the bag label. This applies to attics only. (This labeling procedure is required by law). Shown below is a typical table. The coverage figures will vary according to the manufacturer.

R-Value	Bags per 1000 sq. ft.	Maximum Net Coverage (Sq. Ft.)	Weight Per Sq. Ft. (Lbs.)	Minimum Thickness
R-38	74	14	2.17	13 "
R-30	58	17	1.71	10¼"
R-22	43	24	1.25	7½"
R-19	37	27	1.08	6½"
R-11	22	47	0.63	3¾"

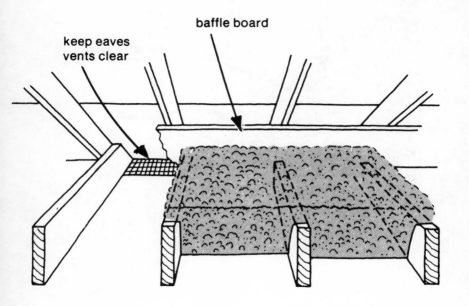

keep eaves vents clear

baffle board

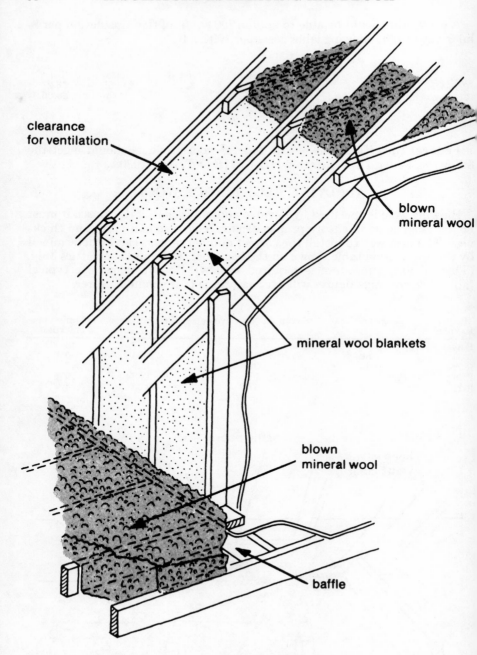

clearance
for ventilation

blown
mineral wool

mineral wool blankets

blown
mineral wool

baffle

The most popular size rock wool blowing insulation comes in 20 lb. bags. Approximate price per bag is $3.50.

Crew size will vary from two to four men or more depending on the size of the job. A minimum crew of two men, with one designated as the lead man is recommended.

Labor To Insulate Attics.—*Unfloored Attics.* Blow three or four joists from one position. Always blow in the direction of the joists and not across them. Be sure that eave vents are not blocked.

Protruding lighting fixtures and fan motors must not be covered with insulation, and insulation must be 3 inches away from their sides. Check both sides of any obstructions. *Floored attics.* It is not advisable to blow more than 4 to 6 feet under flooring. Check for obstructions such as bracing, pipes and electrical conduits. Be sure to fill in and around such obstructions.

Attic knee walls and slopes.— In homes with this type of construction, the easiest method to insulate these areas is with batts or blankets. (For labor and material costs for batts and blankets, see previous section).

Take care to fill any flat areas behind knee walls. If the home includes an attic stairway; the soffit area, the walls and the door should also be insulated. The labor for any of the preceeding is approximately the same and a two-man crew using an open blow, should be able to insulate 7000 sq. ft. using R-19 insulation per 8-hour day, at the following labor cost per 100 sq. ft.:

	Hours	Rate	Total	Rate	Total
Applicator	.11	$. . . .	$. . . .	$13.35	$1.46
Assistant	.11	. . . .	. . . .	$10.60	1.16
Cost per sq. ft.		. . . .	. . . .		$0.03

Labor To Insulate Sidewalls.— All sidewalls are insulated in a similar manner. Openings are made in the sheathing after some of the outside finish has been removed. Insulation is then blown into the empty stud space. It the wall is partially insulated, check the manufacturer to be sure his product is recommended for application in this circumstance. Two openings for sidewalls, called the "double blow" method, are recommended. Some may require three. Openings should be at 4 to 5 foot intervals vertically. This is important in order to completely fill the stud space. Never blow more than 4 feet down or 12 inches up. Special attention should be made to check for obstructions in each stud cavity. Blowing through a single opening in an 8 foot wall could leave much of the stud space with no insulation.

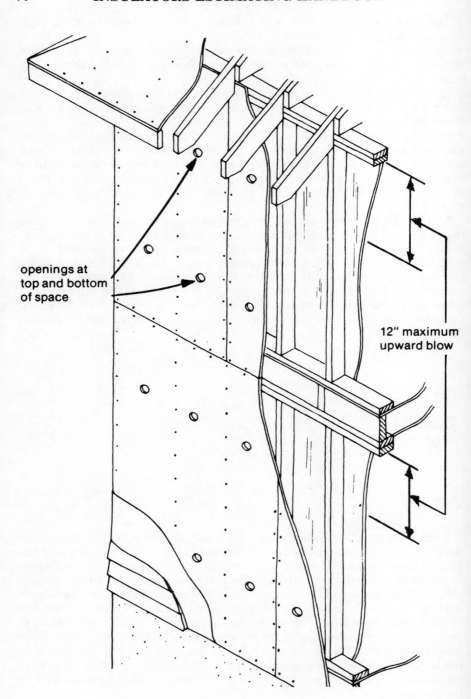

openings at
top and bottom
of space

12" maximum
upward blow

Trim should be removed wherever possible, as this will generally expose studding. A number of homes have eaves which are actually below the level of the plate. Frequently access to the stud space can be gained by removing the eaves panels.

Plumb bob all stud cavities to determine the depth the cavity can be filled. The plumb bob should be of sufficient size to reveal obstructions that would restrict the flow of insulation. Areas under windows and below firestops and bracing must be opened and the area completely filled. After removing nozzle, be sure to hand-pack the area occupied by the nozzle.

Blowing.— Although different applicators have different methods, it is generally recommended that the lower holes be filled first. Otherwise, some lower holes will appear to have been filled from the hole above. The hose should always be inserted in such holes to make sure that the insulation in the lower stud space is of the correct density.

IF A WALL IS PARTIALLY INSULATED, BLOWING WOOL SHOULD NO BE ADDED UNLESS IT IS RECOMMENDED FOR THIS USE BY THE MANUFACTURER.

Machine pressure.— Operational pressures will vary with the job. However, the blowing machine should be equipped with a pop-off valve so that when a section is filled pressure will bleed off at the machine rather than into the wall, eliminating the danger of blowing out the inside wall. Considerably less pressure should be used on a sidewall in which the inner wall is a drywall compared to one which is lath and plaster. Continuous movement of the blowing nozzle will help ensure that an entire cavity is filled. If an opening fills too quickly, check for obstructions. It may be necessary to make another opening below the stoppage.

EXTERIOR SIDEWALL PREPARATION AND APPLICATION

Since the application of blowing wool involves the removal and replacement of outside wall finishes, it is strongly recommended that one member of the crew be a proficient carpenter. For brick or stone, an experienced mason is recommended.

Labor to prepare sidewalls.— Since the labor is approximately the same on all non-masonry walls, a two man crew should be able to remove and replace 500 to 700 sq. ft. of outside finish per 8-hour day at the following labor cost per 100 sq. ft.:

	Hours	Rate	Total	Rate	Total
Applicator	1.33	$....	$....	$13.35	$17.76
Assistant	1.33	....	....	$10.60	14.10
Cost per sq. ft.		....	....		$ 0.32

Interior application should be considered where the exterior is stone, brick or stucco, or the owner is planning to redecorate.

Labor to blow insulation.— Once the outside finish is removed, all sidewalls are insulated in the same manner. Blowing time only, a two-man crew should be able to insulate 300 to 400 sq. ft. of wall per 8-hour day at the following labor cost per 100 sq. ft.:

	Hours	Rate	Total	Rate	Total
Applicator	2.29	$. . . .	$. . . .	$13.35	$30.57
Assistant	2.29	. . . .	. . . .	$10.60	24.27
Cost per sq. ft.		. . . .	. . . .		$ 0.55

Manufacturers.— Among the leading manufacturers of rock wool and slag wool products are:

Owens-Corning Fiberglas Corp., Toledo, OH 43659

United States Gypsum, Chicago, IL 60606

Certainteed Corp., Valley Forge, PA 19482

Johns-Manville Corp., Denver, CO 80217

Rockwool Industries Inc., Denver, CO 80217

U. S. Fiber Corp., Delphos, Ohio 45833

There are also a number of regional manufacturers who make reputable products. Remember, however: "The current issue of the Federal government specification HH-I-1030A requires that each bag of loose-fill material wool insulation be labeled to show the R-value, the number of bags required for 1000 sq. ft. of net attic area; the maximum net sq. ft. coverage of each bag, and the minimum thickness and weight needed to achieve the R-value. The thickness and coverages shown on the bag label, which apply only to open attic insulation, may be different for different manufacturers."

If a manufacturer tries to sell you any material in bags not labeled, don't buy them. There is no way of determining the quality of the product.

Chapter 8

*MINERAL WOOL/***FIBER GLASS**

FIBER GLASS

Fiber glass is a generic term which applies to products of more than one manufacturer. It is different from other mineral wool insulation (rock wool and slag wool) only in the source from which the fibers are spun. There are newer insulation products on the market, yet the popularity of fiber glass continues strong. Even though the physical properties and insulating value of the products of all fiber glass manufacturers are similar, nevertheless, attention should be paid to the specific manufacturer's literature regarding the product, the properties and the intended end use before it is applied.

Manufacturing Process.—Although fiber glass is a member of the mineral wool family of insulation products, it has some characteristics which set it apart. As with mineral wool, the raw materials are of inorganic, mineral origin. Although there are a number of different manufacturing processes, each will fall into one of two major classifications. In the first, molten materials are flowed onto a rapidly spinning rotor bowl. The sidewall contains many holes. As the molten material flows through the holes, high velocity jets form it into relatively short glass fibers.

In the second process, the raw materials are fed in front of high-pressure, high-velocity gas jets forming somewhat longer fibers.

In the remaining steps for both processes, binder is applied, usually phenolic resin, and the treated fibers are collected on a moving belt which passes through the curing oven. The resulting product has a high air content with a low density, typically less than 1.0 lb. per cu. ft., and good thermal characteristics. They also have good resiliency and when compressed tend to return to their original thickness without loss of R-value. Materials for blowing and pouring are commonly produced by hammer milling the blanket materials.

RECOMMENDED INSULATION: CEILING - WALL - FLOOR

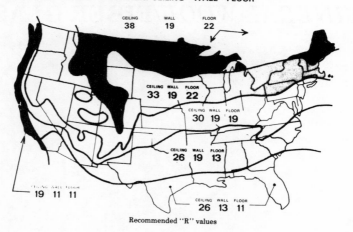

Recommended "R" values

Ceilings, double layers of batts
R-38, Two layers of R-19 (6") mineral fiber
R-33, One layer of R-22 (6½") and one layer of R-11 (3½") mineral fiber
R-30, One layer of R-19 (6") and one layer of R-11 (3½") mineral fiber
R-26, Two layers of R-13 (3-5/8") mineral fiber

Ceilings, loose fill mineral wool and batts
R-38, R-19 (6") mineral fiber and 20 bags of wool per 1,000 S.F. (8¾")
R-33, R-22 (6½") mineral fiber and 11 bags of wool per 1,000 S.F. (5")
R-30, R-19 (6") mineral fiber and 11 bags of wool per 1,000 S.F. (5")

R-26, R-19 (6") mineral fiber and 8 bags of wool per 1,000 S.F. (3¼")

Walls, using 2"x6" framing
R-19, R-19 (6") mineral fiber batts

Walls, using 2"x4" framing
R-19, R-13 (3-5/8") mineral fiber batts and 1" plastic foam sheathing
R-11, R-11 (3½") mineral fiber batts

Floors
R-22, R-22 (6½") mineral fiber
R-19, R-19 (6") mineral fiber
R-13, R-13 (3-5/8") mineral fiber
R-11, R-11 (3½") mineral fiber

Principal Uses.—Fiber glass is used in residential and commercial/industrial building insulation for both new and retrofit applications. Specific applications include ceilings, sidewalls and floors in residential construction, and walls and wood-framed floors in commercial/industrial buildings.

R-Value.—The most commonly used forms of fiber glass insulation are batts and blankets which have a typical R-value of R-3.2 per inch of thickness. Various thicknesses will provide R-values as shown in the following:

Thickness	R-value	Kraft Paper Faced	Foil Faced	Unfaced
1	3.2			X
1-⅛	4			X
1-½	5			X
2-¼-2¾	7	X	X	
3-½-4	11	X	X	
3-5/8	13			X
5	14			X
6-6-½	19	X	X	
7	21	X	X	

For blowing or pouring insulation, the typical R-value is R-2.2 per inch.

Physical Properties.—

Fiberglass

Material Property	Value	Test Method
Density	0.6-1.0 lb/ft^3	
Thermal Conductivity (k factor)	varies with density	
Thermal Resistance (R value) per 1" of thickness* at 75F	3.16 hft^{2}F/Btu (batt) 2.2 hft^{2}F/Btu (loose-fill)	ASTM C518, C653
Water Vapor Permeability	>100 perm-in	
Water Absorption	<1% by weight	ASTM C553-70
Capillarity	none	
Fire Resistance	non-combustible	ASTM E136
Flame Spread	15-20	
Fuel Contributed	5-15	} ASTM E84
Smoke Developed	0-20	
Toxicity	Some toxic fumes could develop due to combustion of binder.	
Effect of Age		
a) Dimensional Stability	none (batt) settling (loose-fill)	
b) Thermal Performance	none	
c) Fire Resistance	none	
Degradation Due To		
Temperature	none below 180°F	
Cycling	none	
Animal	none	
Moisture	none	
Fungal/Bacterial	does not promote growth	
Weathering	none	
Corrosiveness	non-corrosive	Federal HH-I-558D
Odor	none	ASTM C553 - Sec. 16

*Derived from R19 and R11 products for 6 and 3.5" thickness respectively.

Fire Resistance.—Although fiber glass per se is not flammable, the organic materials used to bind it together are. Fiber glass having such binders shows a flame spread average of 15-20, fuel contributed 5-15 and smoke developed 0-20 (ASTM E-84). Asphalt-coated-kraft and foil-kraft paper laminates which are typical facings on fiber glass are also flammable. These facings must not be exposed to open flame or temperatures exceeding 180°F. Ignition of facings or organic binders could produce thermal degredation products which are toxic. Consequently, they should be covered with fire retardant materials (such as ½" gypsum board) when used for thermal insulation. For more specific information consult the manufacturer or manufacturers' literature.

Water Permeability and Moisture Absorption.—Loose fill, batt and blanket fiber glass are permeable to water vapor to the extent of over 100 perm-inch. Water absorption averages no more than 1.0% by weight (ASTM C553-70). No capillarity is apparent.

APPLICATIONS
Fiber Glass Batts and Blankets and Blowing Glass

For most applications, fiber glass batts and blankets are supplied in three forms: foil-faced, kraft-paper faced and unfaced. Other forms of unfaced material are used as sill-sealers and for masonry wall application. Where the materials are faced, the facings act as a vapor barrier. Unfaced material requires a separate vapor barrier. For the actual perm rating of faced material, check the manufacturer or manufacturer's literature. On faced material, the facing projects beyond the fiber glass to form a stapling flange. Unfaced material is friction fit. Application of fiber glass batts is similar to that of mineral wool batts illustrated the previous chapter.

Sizes and Costs.—Blankets and batts are produced in a variety of sizes to fit various construction applications. Batts are generally between 2 ft. and 8 ft. in length, while blankets come in rolls up to 78'4" long. The most common widths are designed to fit between joists, studs and rafters 12-, 16- and 24-inches on center.

Fiber Glass Batts
Material Cost/ Sq. Ft./ Truckload

R-Value	Thickness	Unfaced	Kraft-Faced	Foil-Faced
R-11	3-½-4"	.098	.109	.116
R-13	3-½-4"	.139	.149	
R-19	6-½"	.189	.215	.225
R-22	7-½"	.224	.244	
R-30	9-¼"	.278	.289	

For small lot purchases from lumber yards, add 10-20% to above costs.

Batts are available in the following widths: 11", 15", 16", 19", 23", 24", and lengths of 47", 48", 89", 90", 93", 94", 94-½", 96". Lengths of: 20', 24', 32' and 40' are called blankets.

Labor To Place Fiber Glass Batts and Blankets

New Industrial/Commercial Construction (roofs and ceilings).— An applicator who is accustomed to stapling batts and blankets should be able to place and staple 1000 to 2000 sq. ft. of material per 8-hour day at the following labor cost per 100 sq. ft.:

	Hours	Rate	Total	Rate	Total
Carpenter	.53	$. . . .	$. . . .	$13.35	$7.08
Cost per sq. ft.		. . . .	. . . .		$0.07

New Industrial/Commercial Construction (walls).—An experienced carpenter should be able to staple and place 1500 to 2500 sq. ft. of material on walls 8 ft. or less per 8-hour day at the following labor cost per 100 sq. ft.:

	Hours	Rate	Total	Rate	Total
Carpenter	.40	$. . . .	$. . . .	$13.35	$5.34
Cost per sq. ft.		. . . .	. . . .		$0.05

Retrofit Industrial/Commercial Construction (roofs and ceilings).—Including preparatory work, an experienced carpenter should be able to place and staple 800 to 1600 sq. ft. of material per 8-hour day at the following labor cost per 100 sq. ft.:

	Hours	Rate	Total	Rate	Total
Carpenter	.66	$. . . .	$. . . .	$13.35	$8.89
Cost per sq. ft.		. . . .	. . . .		$0.09

Retrofit Industrial/Commercial Construction (walls).—Including preparatory work, an experienced carpenter should be able to place and staple 1000 to 2000 sq. ft. of material per 8-hour day at the following labor cost per 100 sq. ft.:

	Hours	Rate	Total	Rate	Total
Carpenter	.53	$. . . .	$. . . .	$13.35	$7.07
Cost per sq. ft.		. . . .	. . . .		$0.07

New Residential Construction (roofs and ceilings).—An experienced carpenter should be able to staple and fit 1000 to 1800 sq. ft. of material per 8-hour day at the following labor cost per 100 sq. ft.:

	Hours	Rate	Total	Rate	Total
Carpenter	.57	$. . . .	$. . . .	$13.35	$7.61
Cost per sq. ft.		. . . .	. . . .		$0.08

New Residential Construction (walls).—An experienced carpenter should be able to staple and fit 2000 to 3000 sq. ft. of insulation per 8-hour day at the following labor cost per 100 sq. ft.:

	Hours	Rate	Total	Rate	Total
Carpenter	.32	$. . . .	$. . . .	$13.35	$4.27
					$0.04

New Residential Construction (floors and foundations).—A trained applicator should be able to place and fit 500 to 1000 sq. ft. of material per 8-hour day at the following labor cost per 100 sq. ft.:

	Hours	Rate	Total	Rate	Total
Carpenter	1.07	$. . . .	$. . . .	$13.35	$14.28
Cost per 100 sq. ft.		. . . .	. . . .		$ 0.14

Retrofit Residential Construction (roofs and ceilings).—Including preparatory work, a trained carpenter should be able to place and staple 1000 to 1500 sq. ft. of insulation per 8-hour day at the following labor cost per 100 sq. ft.:

	Hours	Rate	Total	Rate	Total
Carpenter	.64	$. . . .	$. . . .	$13.35	$8.54
Cost per sq. ft.		. . . .	. . . .		$0.09

Retrofit Residential Construction (walls).— Including preparatory work, a trained carpenter should be able to staple and place 1500 to 2500 sq. ft. of insulation material per 8-hour day at the following labor cost per 100 sq. ft.:

	Hours	Rate	Total	Rate	Total
Carpenter	.40	$. . . .	$. . . .	$13.35	$5.34
Cost per sq. ft.		. . . .	. . . .		$0.05

Retrofit Residential Construction (floors and foundations).—Including preparatory work, a trained carpenter should be able to staple and place 415 to 850 sq. ft. of material per 8-hour day at the following labor cost per 100 sq. ft.:

	Hours	Rate	Total	Rate	Total
Carpenter	1.26	$. . . .	$. . . .	$13.35	$16.82
Cost per sq. ft.		. . . .	. . . .		$ 0.17

Codes and Compliances.—Foil faced fiber glass should comply with Federal Specification HH-1-521E, Type III; Kraft-faced material should comply with Federal Specification HH-1-521E, Type II and unfaced material with Federal Specification HH-1-521E, Type I. Fiber glass should also comply with Federal Specification HH-1-558D to be non-corrosive and ASTM C553-Sec. 16 to have no objectionable odor.

APPLYING FIBER GLASS BLOWING WOOL

Like rock wool, fiber glass blowing wool is specified by R-value and not inches of thickness. It must be installed so as to ensure proper density and coverage and minimum thickness. The R-value is dependent upon proper application of the material to the thickness and density recommended by the manufacturer.

The best way to install the correct number of bags can be determined by the application table shown on the bag label. (This is the same labeling procedure required by law for cellulose and other blown mineral wool). Shown below is a typical table.

Coverage figures will vary according to manufacturer and method of installation.

R-Value	Bags per 1000 sq. ft.	Maximum Net Coverage (Sq. Ft.)	Weight Per Sq. Ft. (Lbs.)	Minimum Thickness
R-38	40	25	1.00	13.0''
R-30	32	32	0.78	10.3''
R-22	23	43	0.57	7.5''
R-19	20	50	0.50	6.5''
R-11	12	86	0.29	3.8''

Fiber glass blowing wool is designed for use with standard automatic and hand-fed mineral fiber blowing wool machines. Application is the same as for blown rock wool and slag wool, see pages 61 to 66.

Fiber glass blowing wool comes in 20-, 25-, 30- and 44 lb. bags. Costs vary from approximately $7.50 to $9.00 per bag.

Manufacturers.—The leading manufacturers include Owens-Corning Fiberglas, Toledo OH 43659, Certain-Teed Corporation Valley Forge, PA 19482 and Johns-Manville Corporation, Denver, CO 80217.

Chapter 9

CELLULOSE

CELLULOSE

Cellulose is one of the oldest insulation materials still in common use today. Patents for it's manufacture were issued as early as the 1800's. It is manufactured in three forms, pourable (also called loose-fill), blown-in and sprayed-on. Since the amount of capital investment to become a manufacturer of pourable and blown-in cellulose is low, and the cost of raw materials is low (the basic feed stock is newsprint or wood pulp), the residential business has been plagued with fly-by-night operators. It takes a precise blending of chemicals with the basic feed stock to give cellulose its proper insulating values, as well as inhibit its flammability and corrosiveness, and only "UL Listed" products should be used. If any shortcuts are taken, problems occur. When using cellulose insulation, particular care should be taken to select a reliable manufacturer.

Manufacturing Process.—Cellulose is manufactured by several different processes. Essentially it is made from either used newsprint or paper feedstock. The materials are converted to fibers and treated with certain chemicals to retard flammability.

Dry Process.—This is the original process and is still in common use today. Newsprint is shredded and pulverized into a fibrous reasonably homogeneous material. As the shredded material goes through the final milling process, a dry chemical is usually auger fed directly into the inlet of the mill where it is blended into the fibers. It is then bagged for distribution.

The shredding can be done by a single mill or by multi-mill where it is shredded to confetti size particles and then sent to the holding bin. The holding bin is used to achieve a uniform feed to the last mill. Dry chemicals are mixed with the ground paper at this last stage. This is the most critical step in order to achieve the proper flammability and corrosiveness rating. Without good supervision and quality control at this point, the end product may provide thermal insulation but not meet the criteria set by Federal and Local Regulatory Agencies.

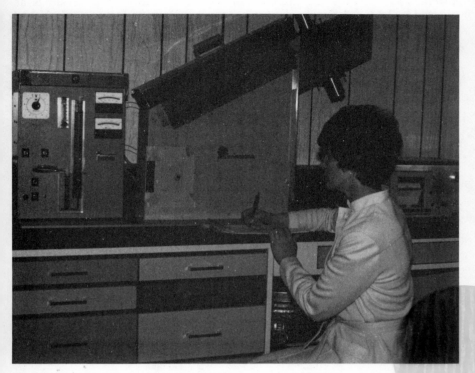

Cellulose should be checked several times daily on an on-going basis in order to be sure that proper chemical dispersion is maintained.

Wet Process.—The first process involves sprinkling or spraying fire retardant chemicals in solution onto the paper stock. This is generally done between the first and second milling operations. Excess moisture is removed in the final milling process through air and a short duration heat build-up developed as it goes through the mill. The amount of chemical and its evaporative characteristics are critical to this process. Too much or too little may result in an inferior to unusable product.

The other wet process utilizes conventional paper making techniques. Paper stock is reduced to a slurry and then dewatered by compression which removes up to 60% of the water. Chemicals are introduced in the slurry stage. The material is then fluffed, dried and bagged.

The wet process offers an alternate method for chemical dispersion which provides better fire retardant characteristics, corrosiveness control and improved resistance to leaching.

Spray-On.—Raw materials are processed in a manner similar to dry materials. Since it is left exposed, it will usually have more fire retardant chemicals, such as boric acid. Binders such as polyvinyl acetate or acrylic adhesive are generally used to bind the material to itself and the substrate. In some applications, adhesive is mixed with water and sprayed onto the product as it leaves the application nozzle. In another, dry resin is activated by water at the nozzle just prior to application. Regardless of which product is used, sprayed-on insulation should only be applied by a trained applicator.

Principal Uses.—The primary use for pourable cellulose is in attics. Pourable and blown-in products which have a Class I rating (flame spread less than 25,) can also be used in a variety of dwelling, schools and commercial low-rise buildings which must use rated materials. Blown-in products can also be used in residential walls, both new and retrofit.

R-Values.—R-values run from R-2.8 to R-3.8 per inch. However, this will vary depending upon the product and how it is used. Newsprint products generally have a higher R-value than products made from other paper or wood pulp. Also, the thicker the material, the lower the R-value per inch. Blown products will have a higher value when blown into an open space, such as an attic floor and a lower R-value when blown into a wall. Even so, 3-½" blown into a wall will have about an R-13 R-value. The coverage chart below shows typical R-values which can be achieved with pourable or blown-in material.

Application Data

Coverages based on 2"X6" Joists - 16" O.C.

R value at 75° mean temp.	Minimum thickness
To obtain an insulation resistance	Installed insulation should not be less
R-40	10.8 inches thick
R-32	8.6 inches thick
R-24	6.5 inches thick
R-19	5.1 inches thick
R-13	3.5 inches thick

Cellulose has a lower R-value if it becomes wet. A vapor barrier is required on the warm-in-winter side.

Physical Properties.—

CELLULOSE

Material Property	Value	Test Method
Density	2.2-3.0 lb/ft^3	
Thermal Conductivity (k factor) at 75F	0.27 to 0.31 Btu-in/ft^{2}hr°F	ASTM C177, C518
Thermal Resistance (R value) per 1" of thickness at 75F	3.7 to 3.2 hft^{2}F/Btu	
Water Vapor Permeability	high	
Water Absorption	5 - 20% by weight	ASTM C739
Capillarity	not known	
Fire Resistance	Combustible	E-136
Flame Spread	15-40	
Fuel Contributed	0-40	ASTM E84
Smoke Developed	0-45	
Toxicity	develops CO when burned	
Effect of Age		
a) Dimensional Stability	settles 0-20%	
b) Thermal Performance	not known	
c) Fire Resistance	inconsistent information	

CELLULOSE—Continued

Material Property	Value	Test Method
Degradation Due To		
Temperature	none	
Cycling	not known	
Animal	not known	
Moisture	not severe	
Fungal/Bacterial	may support growth	
Weathering	not known	
Corrosiveness	may corrode steel, aluminum, copper	ASTM C739
Odor	none	ASTM C739

Fire Resistance.—In 1978, Congress made it mandatory that all cellulose insulation products meet a minimum standard for flame resistance and corrosiveness. Products which meet this standard will carry the following statements on the label: "Attention: This material meets the minimum applicable Federal flammability standard. This standard is based upon laboratory tests only, which do not represent actual conditions which may occur in the home." You should buy only products which carry the preceding statement.

The earliest flame retardant was boric acid which is still in use today. Many other chemicals have been used singly or in combination. These include: boric acid, borax, aluminum sulfate, lime, ammonium sulfate, ammonium phosphate, mono- and diammonium phosphate, aluminum hydrate, aluminum trihydrate and zinc chloride. Preferable are boric acid or borates. Ammonium or sulfates can corrode metal in plumbing or electrical wiring. A flame spread rating of 25 or less is the best for fire resistance. The key to quality products is the UL Classification Mark which should be shown on the bag.

Another important test for flammability is ASTM Designation C-739-77 which shows that a product has been tested and meets the standard specification for Cellulosic Fiber (wood base). Some manufacturers test for flammability, corrosion and conductivity throughout the day. Test results are filed and recorded according to job number. Should there by any questions regarding product performance, copies of the tests can be supplied on all phases of the manufacture of a specific batch of product. For corrosiveness, cellulose should be tested as required by Federal Specification HH-I-515D.

Water Permeability and Moisture Absorption.—Tests have shown that moisture absorption will vary with the manufacturer. Tests have shown that moisture absorption can vary from 5 to 20 percent, but for long term performance should not exceed 15 percent (ASTM C739-73 and HH-I-515).

To protect cellulose from moisture, a vapor barrier should be installed on the warm-in-winter side of homes. (Consult manufacturer's literature and see Chapter on Vapor Barriers). For retrofit, where the material is blown-in, vapor barriers are not used. For sprayed-on material no vapor barrier is required.

APPLICATIONS

Pourable or blown cellulose should not be used where temperatures will exceed 180°F. Attic vents should not be covered. Insulation must be kept a minimum of 3" from chimney flues, recessed lighting fixtures, wires and other heating elements.

Pourable cellulose is specified by R-value and not inches of thickness. It must be installed so as to ensure proper density, coverage and minimum thickness. The best way to install the correct number of bags can be determined by the application table shown on the bag label. This applies to attics only. (This labeling procedure is required by law). Shown below is a typical table. The coverage figures will vary according to the manufacturer.

Application Data

Coverages based on
2" x 6" Joists - 16" O.C.
30 lb. bags

R value at 75° mean temp.	Minimum thickness	Maximum net coverage		Minimum weight per sq. ft.
To obtain an insulation resistance of	Installed insulation should not be less than	Maximum sq. ft. coverage per bag	Bags per 1000 sq. ft. (gross)	The weight per sq. ft. of installed be not less than:
R-40	10.8 inches thick	14.0 square feet	71.4 bags/MSF	2.14 lbs./sq. ft.
R-32	8.6 inches thick	17.8 square feet	56.2 bags/MSF	1.69 lbs./sq. ft.
R-24	6.5 inches thick	24.4 square feet	41.0 bags/MSF	1.23 lbs./sq. ft.
R-19	5.1 inches thick	31.9 square feet	31.3 bags/MSF	0.94 lbs./sq. ft.
R-13	3.5 inches thick	45.5 square feet	22.0 bags/MSF	0.66 lbs./sq. ft.

For coverage of a specific product consult the manufacturer or the manufacturer's literature.

Pourable and blown cellulose comes in 20, 30 and 40 lb. bags. Costs per bag are $2.85 to $3.16/20 lb., $4.30 to $4.75/30 lb., and $5.75 to $6.35/40 lb.

Crew size will vary from two to four men or more depending upon the size of the job. A minimum crew of two men, with one designated lead man is recommended.

POURABLE CELLULOSE

Labor To Place Pourable Cellulose.—(Attics and Ceilings in commercial and residential construction, new and retrofit).

An applicator and assistant should be able to place 700 to 900 sq. ft. per 8-hour day at a thickness of 3½" to 3⅝" at the following labor cost per 100 sq. ft.:

	Hours	Rate	Total	Rate	Total
Applicator	1	$....	$....	$13.35	$13.35
Assistant	1	....	....	$10.60	$10.60
Cost per sq. ft.		....	....		$ 0.24

BLOWN CELLULOSE

Labor To Insulate Attics. Unfloored Attics.—Blow three or four joists from one position. Blow in the direction of the joists and not across them. Be sure that eaves are not blocked, and material is not close to installations which could create a fire hazard. A two-man crew should be able to blow approximately 4800 sq. ft. to a depth of R-19 per 8-hour day at the following labor costs per 100 sq. ft.:

	Hours	Rate	Total	Rate	Total
Applicator	.16	$. . . .	$. . . .	$13.35	$ 2.14
Assistant	.16	. . . .	. . . .	$10.60	$ 1.70
Cost per sq. ft.		. . . .	. . . .		$ 0.04

Cellulose should be blown in the direction of the joists and not across them.

Check both sides of any obstructions. *Floored Attics.* It is not advisable to blow more than 4 to 6 feet per hole under flooring. Drilling holes for blowing, and closing holes, is approximately $0.10 per hole. Check for obstructions such as bracing, pipes and electrical conduits. A two-man crew should be able to blow approximately 3600 sq. ft. of attic per 8-hour day at the following labor cost per 100 sq. ft.:

	Hours	Rate	Total	Rate	Total
Applicator	.22	$. . . .	$. . . .	$13.35	$2.94
Assistant	.22	. . . .	. . . .	$10.60	$2.33
Cost per sq. ft.		. . . .	. . . .		$0.05

Attic knee walls and slopes.—In homes with this type of construction, the easiest method to insulate these areas is with batts and blankets.

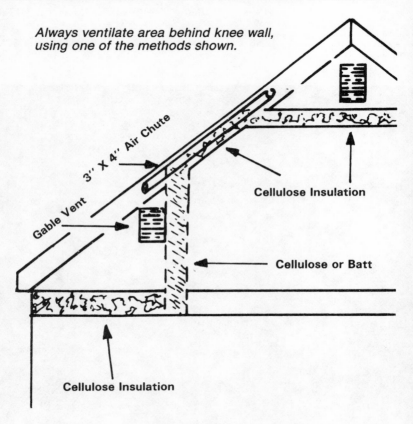

Always ventilate area behind knee wall, using one of the methods shown.

3" X 4" Air Chute

Gable Vent

Cellulose Insulation

Cellulose or Batt

Cellulose Insulation

Be sure to fill any flat areas behind the knee wall. If the home includes an attic stairway; the soffit area, the walls and door should also be insulated. The labor for any of the preceeding is approximately the same and a two-man crew should be able to blow 1200 to 1500 sq. ft. per 8-hour day at the following labor cost per 100 sq. ft.:

	Hours	Rate	Total	Rate	Total
Applicator	.6	$. . . .	$. . . .	$13.35	$8.01
Assistant	.6	. . . .	. . . .	$10.60	$6.36
Cost per sq. ft.		. . . .	. . . .		$0.14

Labor To Insulate Sidewalls.—All sidewalls are insulated in a similar manner. Openings are made in the sheathing after some of the outside finish has been removed. Insulation is then blown into the empty stud space. If the wall is partially insulated, check the manufacturer to be sure his product is recommended for application in this circumstance. Two openings for sidewalls, called the "double blow" method, are recommended. Some may require three. Openings should be at 4 to 5 foot intervals vertically. This is important in order to completely fill the stud space.

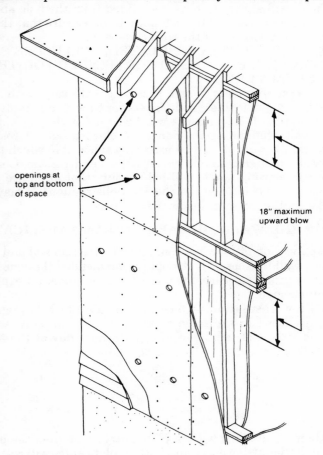

openings at top and bottom of space

18" maximum upward blow

Never blow more than 4 feet down or 12 inches up. Special attention should be made to check for obstructions in each stud cavity. Blowing through a single opening in an 8 foot wall could leave much of the stud space with no insulation.

Trim should be removed wherever possible, as this will generally expose studding. A number of homes have eaves which are actually below the level of the plate. Access to the stud space may often be gained by removing the eaves panels.

Plumb bob all stud cavities to determine the depth to which the cavity can be filled. The plumb bob should be of sufficient size to reveal obstructions that would restrict the flow of insulation. Areas under windows and below firestops and bracing must be opened and the area competely filled. After removing nozzle, be sure to hand-pack the area occupied by the nozzle.

Blowing.—Although different applicators have different methods, it is generally recommended that the lower holes be filled first. Otherwise, some lower holes will appear to have been filled from the hole above. The hose should always be inserted in such holes to make sure that the insulation in the lower stud space is of the correct density.

IF A WALL IS PARTIALLY INSULATED, CELLULOSE SHOULD NOT BE ADDED UNLESS IT IS RECOMMENDED FOR THIS USE BY THE MANUFACTURER.

Machine Pressure.—Operational pressures will vary with the job. However, the blowing machine should be equipped with a pop-off valve so that when a section is filled pressure will bleed off at the machine rather than into the wall, eliminating the danger of blowing out the inside wall. Considerably less pressure should be used on a sidewall in which the inner wall is a drywall compared to one which is lath and plaster. Continuous movement of the blowing nozzle will help ensure that an entire cavity is filled. If an opening fills too quickly, check for obstructions. It may be necessary to make another opening below the stoppage.

EXTERIOR SIDEWALL PREPARATION AND APPLICATION

Since the application of blowing wool involves the removal and replacement of outside wall finishes, it is strongly recommended that one member of the crew be a proficient carpenter. For brick or stone, an experienced mason is recommended.

Labor To Blow Insulation.—Once the outside finish is prepared all sidewalls are insulated in the same manner. A two-man crew should be able to insulate 1000–1200 sq. ft. of wall per 8-hour day at the following labor cost per 100 sq. ft.:

	Hours	Rate	Total	Rate	Total
Applicator	.73	$. . . .	$. . . .	$13.35	$9.75
Assistant	.73	. . . .	. . . .	$10.60	$7.74
Cost per sq. ft.		. . . .	. . . .		$0.17

An alternate method is the bottom plate entry, done from the basement or crawl space. Both outside entry and bottom plate entry will cost approximately the same.

Model Building Codes.—All cellulose products should meet or exceed the following standard: Federal Specification HH-I-515D and be UL Listed.

Manufacturers.—Among the leading manufacturers of cellulose insulation who distribute nationally are U. S. Fiber, Delphos, Ohio 45833; Electra Mfg. Corp., Holland (Toledo) Ohio 43528; Diversified Ins. Inc., Hamel, Minn. 55340; and Scientific Applications, Inc., Mt. Pleasant, Iowa 52641.

There are also a number of regional manufacturers who make reputable products. Remember, however: "The current issue of the Federal Government Specification HH-I-515D requires that each bag of loose-fill cellulose insulation be labeled to show the R-value, the number of bags required for 1000 sq. ft. of net attic area; the maximum net sq. ft. coverage of each, and the minimum thickness and weight needed to achieve the R-value. The thickness and coverages shown on the bag label, which apply only to attic floor insulation, may be different for different manufacturers." If a product is not labeled, don't buy it.

Chapter 10

PERLITE/VERMICULITE

PERLITE AND VERMICULITE

While there are several kinds of insulation materials which can be extracted or mined, the best known are perlite and vermiculite.

Both are silicates. Perlite is a generic term for naturally occurring siliceous volcanic rock. Unprocessed, it is a glass-like material composed of aluminum silicate with a concentric shelly structure, usually greyish and crystalline in appearance. Vermiculite is a mineral consisting of aluminum-iron-magnesium silicates.

Manufacturing Process.—Both are obtained by strip mining, and processed by crushing, sorting (screening for size) and furnacing. Crushed perlite ore particles are expanded from 4 to 20 times their original size by rapidly heating them to a temperature of 1000°C. This vaporizes the water and forms vapor cells in the heat softened glass.

When vermiculite is subjected to a temperature of approximately 800°C., it expands due to the formation of steam. A wide range of densities is available up to 20 times the original size. The reason for this is the variety of vermiculite ores available and the intrinsic differences between them. Both are mined primarily in the United States.

Principal Uses.—Perlite and vermiculite are used primarily as loose fill insulation in concrete block and hollow wall construction. They can also be used to insulate attics, lofts and sidewalls. Perlite became famous as the white aggregate used as a sand substitute in lightweight gypsum and Portland cement plaster. With the increased popularity of gypsum wall board, however, much of that market has deteriorated. It still maintains its fame as a low temperature insulator.

Vermiculite, while used more widely as a loose fill attic insulation, is best known perhaps as the fire retarding agent in sprayable direct-to-steel plaster and cement.

All vermiculite is a mica. The type of vermiculite and the identification of particulate matter that results from processing it is traceable directly back to the type of vermiculite being used. Perlite, while found in less variable forms, is composed primarily of aluminum silicate.

Vermiculite dust, depending on the type of ore, contains traceable asbestos which can become airborne during certain phases of installation. Perlite contains no asbestos.

Because both perlite and vermiculite are silicates, when they are being manufactured and installed they can shed airborne silicone particles. In the case of perlite, dust suppressing chemicals are added to the coating of the beads. Vermiculite, while not known for the problem, will also produce an airborne residue from the bagged product. Research is continuing to determine what, if any, corrective action should be taken.

R-Values.—Multiply the stated "R" value of one inch of either product by the number of inches needed to achieve the thermal rating desired. Research indicates that neither product experiences the "R" value "fall-off" as thickness increases, as is found with some insulation products. Shown below are the R-values of a number of uninsulated masonry materials whose R-values can be raised substantially through the use of perlite or vermiculite.

R-Values of Common Masonry Materials
(Uninsulated)

Materials	Thickness (Inches)	R-Value
Sand and gravel concrete	8"	1.11
block	12"	1.28
Lightweight concrete	8"	2.00
block	12"	2.13
Face brick	4"	.44
Cast-in-place concrete	8"	.64

Physical Properties.—

VERMICULITE

Material Property	Loose-Fill	Vermiculite Concrete	Test Method
Density	4 to 10 lb/ft^3	20 to 60 lb/ft^3	
K_{app} at 75F	0.33-0.41	0.59-0.96	ASTM C177
	Btu-in/ft^{2}hF	Btu-in/ft^{2}hF	
Thermal Resistance (R value)	3.0-2.4	1.7-1.0	
per 1" of thickness at 75F	hrft^{2}F/Btu	hft^{2}F/Btu	
Water Vapor Permeability	high	high	
Water Absorption	none	none	
Capillarity	none	none	
Fire Resistance	non-combustible	non-combustible	ASTM E136
Flame Spread	0	0	
Fuel Contributed	0	0	
Smoke Developed	0	0	ASTM E84
Toxicity	none	none	
Effect of Age			
a) Dimensional Stability	none	none	
b) Thermal Performance	none	none	
c) Fire Resistance	none	none	
Degradation Due To			
Temperature	none below 1000F	none below 1000F	
Cycling	none	none	
Animal	none	none	
Moisture	none	none	
Fungal/Bacterial	does not promote growth	does not promote growth	
Weathering	none	none	
Corrosiveness	none	none	
Odor	none	none	

PERLITE

Material Property	Value		Test Method
	Loose-Fill	Perlite Concrete	
Density	2-11 lb/ft³	20-40 lb/ft³	
K_{app} at 75F	0.27-0.40	0.50-0.93	ASTM C-177
	Btu-in/ft²hr°F	Btu-in/ft²hr°F	
Thermal Resistance (R value)	3.7-2.5	2.0-1.08	
per 1" thickness at 75F	hft²F/Btu	hft²F/Btu	
Water Vapor Permeability	high	high	
Water Absorption	low		
Capillarity			
Fire Resistance	non-combustible	non-combustible	ASTM E136
Flame Spread	0	0	
Fuel Contributed	0	0	ASTM E84
Smoke Developed	0	0	
Toxicity	not toxic	not toxic	
Effect of Age			
a) Dimensional Stability	none	none	
b) Thermal Performance	none	none	
c) Fire Resistance	none	none	
Degradation Due To			
Temperature	none under 1200°F	none under 500°F	
Cycling	none	none	
Animal	none	none	
Moisture	none	none	
Fungal/Bacterial	does not promote growth	does not promote growth	
Weathering	none	none	
Corrosiveness	none	none	
Odor	none	none	

Fire Resistance.—Both are non-combustible.

Water Permeability and Moisture Absorption.—Perlite and vermiculite have high water permeability. Water absorption is low to none, as is capillarity. Vermiculite is treated with silicone for added water repellency.

Courtesy Perlite Institute, Inc.

Dust suppressed perlite attic insulation may be applied by blowing (as shown above) or by pouring directly from bags to the required depth.

APPLICATIONS

Insulating Attics and Sidewalls.—Vermiculite is marketed in 4 cu. ft. bags costing approximately $3.60 per bag. Approximate coverage per bag based on joists 16" o.c. is 14 sq. ft. for a 3-5/8" thickness, 9 sq. ft. for a 5-1/2" thickness.

When adequate ventilation is provided in attics or similar spaces it is not necessary to use a vapor barrier in ceiling construction below vermiculite. A vapor barrier is recommended on the warm side of insulated exterior walls except when the insulated space is ventilated to permit movement of water vapor and air from the space. A satisfactory vapor barrier may be obtained by painting the interior surface of the wall with a good vapor barrier paint.

Insulating Cavity and Block Walls.—Both vermiculite and perlite can be used in this application. Coverage and costs are about the same.

Approximate Coverage of Vermiculite Fill in Cavity and Block Walls

Sq. ft. wall area	1" cavity	2" cavity	2½" cavity	8" block	12" block
100	2 bags*	4 bags*	5 bags*	7 bags*	13 bags*
500	10 "	20 "	25 "	34 "	63 "
1,000	21 "	42 "	50 "	69 "	125 "
5,000	104 "	208 "	250 "	545 "	625 "
10,000	208 "	416 "	500 "	1,090 "	1,250 "

*1 bag=4 cu. ft.

Courtesy Perlite Institute, Inc.

Silicone treated perlite loose-fill insulation being poured in cores of concrete block wall. The free-flowing material completely fills every crevice within the cavity.

Installation is usually done by a mason. One mason can pour around 50 bags or 200 cu. ft. per 8-hour day at the following labor costs per 100 cu. ft.:

Labor Cost per 100 cu.ft.

	Hours	Rate	Total	Rate	Total
Mason	4	$. . . .	$. . . .	13.12	$52.48
Labor cost per cu. ft.		. . . .	. . . .		$ 0.53

Material Cost Per 100 cu. ft.

25 ea. 4 cu. ft. bags @ $3.60 ea.	=	$90.00
Material cost per cu. ft.		$ 0.90

Combined Material & Labor Cost per 100 cu. ft.

Labor $52.48 plus Material $90.00	=	$142.48
Combined cost per cu. ft.		$ 1.43

Cost of material for insulating an 8" x 8" x 16" concrete block is about $0.20 per sq. ft. of wall surface. For a cavity wall, $0.075 per bd. ft. Installation cost is about $0.036 per sq. ft. of wall surface.

Model Building Codes.—None required. However, applicators should check local building codes to see if any apply.

Manufacturers.—W. R. Grace, Construction Products Division, Cambridge, Mass. 02140; American Vermiculite Corp., Atlanta, Ga. 30329.

Chapter 11

ROOFING

ROOFING

Historically, roofing was laid essentially to provide waterproofing. In residential construction, insulation, if any, was generally put in the attic. In commercial construction, it was generally placed on the underside of the roof, inside the building.

Today, however, the situation is rapidly changing. The advent of "A" frame construction, exposed beam, vaulted and cathedral ceilings pose a real problem for builders. With the energy losses which can occur with such construction, builders were forced to look for new solutions.

In commercial construction, placing insulation on the inside was seldom satisfactory. In addition, with conventional BUR (Built Up Roofing) systems, water frequently ponded on the roof, adding to the woes of the building owners and occupants.

As a result, two new systems have evolved utilizing insulation materials which provide solutions to these problems in both residential and commercial construction.

In residential construction, roofers are now placing insulation over the roof decking on the outside. In commercial construction, they are doing the same thing, except that they are tapering the insulation material so that after the BUR system is placed over the insulation, the flow of water can be directed and controlled so as to eliminate ponding.

INSULATING EXPOSED BEAM CEILINGS

Products which can be used for this application include expanded polystyrene, Styrofoam, urethane and isocyanurate. Since the application procedure can vary according to product, the manufacturer should be consulted prior to application. Roofers should also determine that the product being applied meets local building codes. Lay only as much insulation as can be covered by the BUR system in the same day.

The following procedure utilizes expanded polystyrene.

Apply the insulation over a nailable deck with a slope of three inches in twelve inches or greater. Install a wood nailer at eaves, overhangs and valleys wherever flashings or gravel stops are to be attached. The nailer should be the same thickness as the insulation. Nail or staple insulation to the deck and cover with 15 lb. asphalt impregnated roofing felt laid perpendicular to the slope, starting at the bottom. Using standard application procedures, lap felt four inches at the ends and two inches at edges and nail or staple to hold until shingles are applied.

Nail shingles in accordance with manufacturer's specifications using galvanized nails of sufficient length to penetrate the deck ¾ inches. Be sure to drive nails square and flush so heads do not cut shingles.

A roofer and assistant should be able to place about 2,000 sq. ft. of insulation and roofing shingles per 8-hour day at the following labor cost for 100 sq. ft.:

	Hours	Rate	Total	Rate	Total
Roofer	.4	$. . . .	$. . . .	$12.66	$5.06
Assistant	.4	. . . .	. . . .	$10.60	4.24
Labor Cost per sq. ft.		. . . .	. . . .		.09
Material Cost per sq. ft.		. . . .	. . . .		.40
Combined Labor and Material Cost per sq. ft.		. . . .	. . . .		.49

For special considerations such as slopes greater than 4 inches in 12 inches or less than 3 inches in 12 inches or special finishes, the insulation manufacturer should be contacted. NOTE: Some systems require a ½ inch plywood be laid over the insulation (see insulation manufacturer's specs.) to act as a nailing base for the roofing material.

Shingle Overdeck

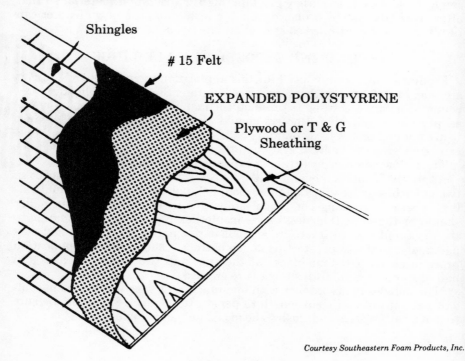

Shingles

15 Felt

EXPANDED POLYSTYRENE

Plywood or T & G
Sheathing

Courtesy Southeastern Foam Products, Inc.

TAPERED ROOFS

As with the overdeck insulation system just described, the tapered system can be placed utilizing expanded polystyrene, perlite board, urethane and cellular glass. Since there can be variations as to the way individual products are applied, applicators should check with the manufacturer as to the proper procedure. In some cases the manufacturer will prepare the roof insulation plan for approval by the specifier.

Systems can be designed to go over any roof deck, as well as meet codes and insurance requirements. This type of roofing offers the designer the latitude to meet almost any thermal resistance needed in either flat or slope-to-drain tapered insulation.

Tapered systems are composed of pre-cut, and in the case of one manufacturer, color-coded, ready-to-install tapered boards. Other systems number the boards.

SIMPLIFIED TAPERED INSULATION LAY-UP

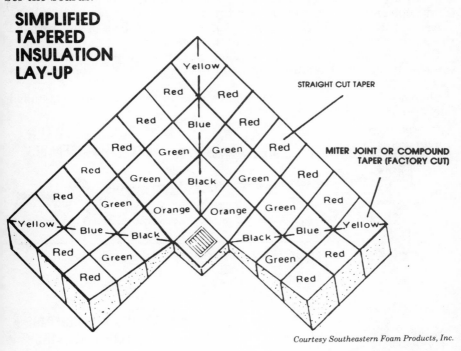

STRAIGHT CUT TAPER

MITER JOINT OR COMPOUND TAPER (FACTORY CUT)

Courtesy Southeastern Foam Products, Inc.

The single layer system is furnished from some manufacturers; from others the system will need multiple layers to accomplish proper drainage. A system may consist of predesigned modules having a slope of ⅛", ¼", ⅜" or ½" per foot as required.

When planning the proper slope, The Asphalt Roofing Manufacturers Association, The National Roofing Contractors Association and most roofing materials manufacturers recommend that the minimum slope be ¼" to the foot to allow for proper drainage.

The slope chart below will aid in determining the proper slope to drain.

SLOPE CHART

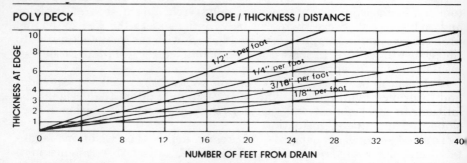

There are two types of modules available. A standard module with a uniform slope and a corner module with two slopes.

Enough slope should be built in so water does not collect in any area and there is no standing water 24 hours after rainfall.

Drains should be located at low points, preferably in sumps. The system can also be designed to direct water flow to parapet wall scuppers or gutters.

Shown below are three typical applications, in this case using expanded polystyrene.

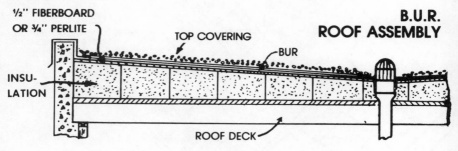

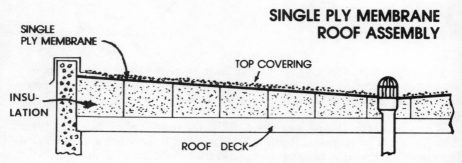

Courtesy Southeastern Foam Products, Inc.

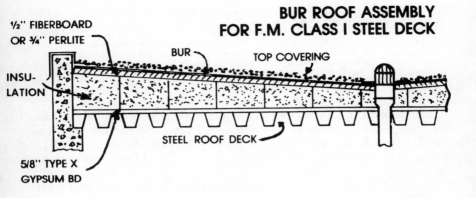

BUR ROOF ASSEMBLY FOR F.M. CLASS I STEEL DECK

½" FIBERBOARD OR ¾" PERLITE

BUR — TOP COVERING

INSULATION

STEEL ROOF DECK

5/8" TYPE X GYPSUM BD

R-VALUE	PRODUCT DESCRIPTION	SIZES
R Value: 4.17 per inch Thickness	A 1.00 pound per cubic foot density expanded polystyrene foam (modified grade) meeting Federal Specification HH-I-524b, Type I, Class A. Available flat or in slope-to-drain boards with ⅛", ¼", ⅜", or ½" per foot taper.	4'x4' Thickness-½" to 16" in ⅛" increments
R Value: 4.33 per inch Thickness	A 1.25 pound per cubic foot density expanded polystyrene foam (modified grade) meeting Federal Specification HH-I-524b, Type I, Class A. Available flat or in slope-to-drain boards with ⅛", ¼", ⅜" or ½" per foot taper.	4'x4' Thickness-½" to 16" in ⅛" increments
R Value: 4.55 per inch Thickness	A 1.50 pound per cubic foot density expanded polystyrene foam (modified grade) meeting Federal Specification HH-I-524b, Type II, Class A. Available flat or in slope-to-drain boards with ⅛", ¼", ⅜", or ½" per foot taper.	4'x4' Thickness-½" to 16" in ⅛" increments

USE RECOMMENDATIONS
TAPERED OR FLAT

		100	125	150	PF 100	PF 125	PF 150
ROOF DECKS	Metal	Yes	Yes	Yes	Yes	Yes	Yes
	Concrete	Yes	Yes	Yes	Yes	Yes	Yes
	Wood	Yes	Yes	Yes	Yes	Yes	Yes
ADHESIVES	Asphalt	Yes	Yes	Yes	Yes	Yes	Yes
	Coal Tar Pitch	No	No	No	No	No	No
	Asphalt Emulsion	Yes	Yes	Yes	Yes	Yes	Yes
	Cold Adhesive	Yes (1)	Yes (1)	Yes (1)	Yes (1)	Yes (1)	Yes(1)
	Mechanical Fastening	Yes (2)	Yes (2)	Yes (2)	Yes (2)	Yes (2)	Yes(2)
MEMBRANES	Asphaltic B.U.R.	Yes (3)	Yes (3)	Yes (3)	No	No	No
	Coal Tar Pitch B.U.R.	No	No	No	No	No	No
	Loose Laid Single Ply	Yes	Yes	Yes	Yes (4)	Yes (4)	Yes (4)
	Adhered Single Ply	Yes	Yes	Yes	Yes	Yes	Yes
	Liquid Applied	Yes (5)	Yes (5)	Yes (5)	Yes (5)	Yes (5)	Yes (5)
	U.L. Rated (File R7260)	Yes	Yes	Yes	—	—	—
	FM Class I - Metal Deck	—	Yes (6)	Yes (6)	—	—	—

(1) Confirm from Manufacturer capability with expanded polystyrene foam
(2) Follow fastener use recommendations
(3) Use top layer over Poly Deck (a) ¾" Perlite Board or (b) ½" Fiberboard as base to receive B.U.R.
(4) Designed for single ply membranes, loose laid, or adhered systems requiring slip sheets
(5) Confirm with membrane manufacturer compatibility with expanded polystyrene foam
(6) Product meets FM Class I requirements when ⅝" Type X Gypsum Board is applied to metal deck as a substrate for the Poly Deck Insulation - See FM-1979 Approval Guide p. 429 for details.

In applying the tapered system, modules are laid in parallel courses with the long joints continuous and the end joints broken. The edges of the boards are butted firmly to adjoining boards. Install only as much insulation in one day as can be covered by the completed roof system that same day.

The system may be used with asphaltic BUR membrane and single-ply membranes.

A roofer and assistant can lay about 1500 sq. ft. of tapered insulation and BUR per 8-hour day at the following labor cost per 100 sq. ft.:

	Hours	Rate	Total	Rate	Total
Roofer	.5	$....	$....	$12.66	$6.33
Assistant	.5	....	....	$10.60	5.30
Labor cost per sq. ft.		....	....		.12
Material cost per sq. ft.		....	....		1.20
Combined labor and material cost per sq. ft.		....	....		1.32

Manufacturers. Benoit, Inc., St. Paul, MN 55104; Southeastern Foam Products, Conyers GA 30207; Western Insulfoam Corp., Seattle, WA; Contour Packaging, Inc., Kansas City, MO 64108 and Toyad Corp., Latrobe, PA 15650.

Chapter 12

VAPOR BARRIERS

VAPOR BARRIERS

Vapor barriers are water-proofing membranes which are an integral part of the insulation material added on to the structural framing. Their purpose is to restrict the migration of moisture to the insulation or structural members.

Generally, vapor barriers and properly vented walls are required where the climate indicates winter condensation problems. You can expect these problems wherever the average temperature in January falls below 35°F. As you can see in the illustration, this can occur in approximately two thirds of the country.

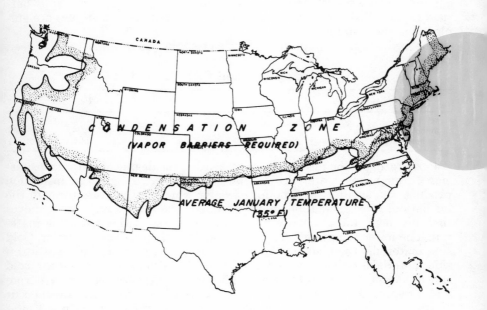

In an average home, as many as 20 gallons of water per week are transmitted into the air. In mild climates, where open windows and doors produce adequate ventilation, this moisture provides no particular problem. In residential or commercial structures sealed for energy conservation, however, a measurably destructive percentage of this normal condensation will go through the walls, ceilings and floors and infiltrate the insulation, unless proper protective measures are taken.

The ideal vapor barrier is designed to completely stop the movement of moisture. Examples of this type of impermeability are found in foil or membrane covered materials as well as in some coatings which can be applied to existing insulation of high permeability.

There are also integral barriers such as stainless steel and closed cell insulation which fall into this category. These are usually an integral part of the building envelope or are used for structural integrity.

Ironically, the improvement of insulation materials and techniques of installation, some of which produce a virtually "void-proof" job have radically reduced ventilation. Even though this was done in the interest of energy conservation, it has made the installation of effective vapor barriers even more important. Recently enacted Federal Legislation concerning permeability could expose the contractor to legal liability in the case of faulty materials or installation.

ASHRAE (The American Society of Heating, Refrigeration and Air Conditioning Engineers) suggests that vapor barriers be installed on the "warm-in-winter" side of the wall and that the barriers be as "void-free" as possible. Since nearly all vapor barriers are penetrated by wires, vents, conduits or ductwork, ASHRAE recommends that secondary vapor barriers be installed even when such small void producers as staples are employed in the installation.

The reduction of impermeability caused by such voids can be seen below.

Based on Foil and Foil Laminate

Condition	Perms
As received	0.02
35 pinholes per ft. 2	0.04
A few holes larger than pinholes	0.08-0.16

Perm rating is the term used for measuring the degree of water transmission through any material. The lower the perm rating of an insulation product, the smaller the amount of water which can migrate through the insulation. Most insulations have a tendency to absorb water as it moves through them, thereby lowering the effectiveness of the insulating material. The lower the perm rating, the more effective the vapor barrier. Cold side materials, then, should have a much higher perm rating than warm side materials, because most harmful condensation occurs when the cold side of a building begins to warm. This happens because vapor moves from high pressure to low pressure areas. Condensation of the vapors will occur at any point where the local temperature is *below* the local dew point temperature.

PROPER PLACEMENT OF VAPOR BARRIERS

Building Section	Acceptable	Not Acceptable
Garage wall	vapor barrier / approved interior finish	exposed vapor barrier
Floor above crawl space	conditioned space / vapor barrier / mechanical attachment	conditioned space / vapor barrier
Floor of unfinished attic	ceiling / vapor barrier	exposed vapor barrier / ceiling
Pitched roof	vapor barrier / approved interior finish	exposed vapor barrier
Roof above suspended ceiling	vapor barrier / ceiling system	exposed vapor barrier / ceiling system

Illustration courtesy MIMA

Vapor barriers are extremely important when using cellulose materials; because when exposed to water or conditions which may result in the condensation of water, the chemicals may leach out over a period of time.

With one exception, vapor barriers are placed on the inside of the insulation material between studs or other frame members. The exception is where a barrier is used in slab-on-grade construction. Then the vapor barrier is placed on the *outside* of the insulation to protect it from ground moisture.

When condensation infiltrates the insulation, two things can happen: 1) Thermal resistance is greatly reduced and; 2) Over a period of time, many structural materials will suffer degradation—some to the point of rotting. As a basic reference, the materials list at the end of this chapter show the perm rating of many basic insulation materials in use today.

Unfortunately, no *one* reliable method has been found to predict effective permeability in any given circumstance, so direct testing is recommended where there is doubt as to what material should be applied as a vapor barrier. Because tests at intermediate humidities are difficult and not generally practical, the wet and dry cup* methods are used as an easier way to test for water vapor transmission.

Permeance and Resistance of
Materials to Water Vapor (Dry Cup Method)

Material	Permeance (Perm)	Resistance (Rep)
Plastic and metal foils and films		
Aluminum foil (1 mil)	0.0	
Aluminum foil (0.35 mil)	0.05	20
Polyethylene (2 mil)	0.16	6.3
Polyethylene (4 mil)	0.08	12.5
Polyethylene (6 mil)	0.06	17
Polyethylene (8 mil)	0.04	25
Polyethylene (10 Mil)	0.03	33
Polyester (1 mil)	0.7	1.4
Cellulose acetate (125 Mil)	0.4	2.5
Polyvinylchloride, unplasticized (2 mil)	0.68	1.5
Polyvinylchloride plasticized (4 mil)	0.8-1.4	1.3-0.72

Vapor barrier choice is also determined by a number of external factors. Where moisture accumulation takes place on an annual basis, as in heated buildings, the barrier is not as critical as one needed for a cold storage unit. A house without sheathing will require a better barrier than one which is sheathed, Pre-fabricated structures with only metal sheeting outside the insulation require a vapor barrier of very high resistance on the warm side. The severity of the winters and the interior pressure of the structure must also be taken into consideration.

The best time to vapor-proof a building is during construction. Many retrofit problems which show up later can be traced directly to moisture problems. They range from bubbled walls, to walls peeled by moisture, to

---

*ASHRAE "1977 Fundamentals Handbook"

water-rot induced structural damage. Retrofit installation of vapor barriers can be extremely costly and is usually unnecessary where proper preplanning is done.

The most commonly used vapor barrier is polyethylene sheeting in 4- or 6-mil thicknesses. Price per sq. ft. for 4-mil is approximately $0.03 and for 6-mil $0.04. Both sizes come in 100 ft. rolls. The widths and approximate prices per roll are shown below:

4-mil		6-mil	
Width	Price	Width	Price
8 ft.	$12.15	10 ft.	$22.81
10 ft.	15.18	12 ft.	27.33
12 ft.	18.23	14 ft.	31.89
16 ft.	24.30	16 ft.	36.44
20 ft.	30.37	20 ft.	45.56

Choose the thickness which best suits the job, keeping in mind its perm rating and the duration of moisture producing conditions. When structural limitations make void free installation impossible, don't be afraid to use a second or third barrier—it will be well worth the effort.

Chapter 13

THERMOGRAPHY

THERMOGRAPHY

The requirement that insulation be "void free" is being written into more and more construction contracts, both residential and commercial. End users of structures are becoming more aware of insulation as an integral part of construction because of recently enacted tax advantages of energy savings through insulation. Equally important, in many instances, if the insulation job does not meet established or contractural standards, the applicator and/or contractor can be held legally liable.

The only scientific method available to check the quality of insulation without going into the walls is thermography. Thermography shows, in the form of pictures, or electronically produced video images, where there is a void in already installed insulation. It does so by converting invisible thermal radiation into visible light and recording it.

Infrared or thermal radiation occupies a portion of the light spectrum that is invisible to the human eye. The thermographic imaging device simply makes it possible to "see" and identify thermal radiation or temperature leakage from a given structure.

Infrared or thermographic scanning is available as a tool to save time and money for the insulation contractor and the consumer. It can be used while the job is being done to check specification compliance and find problem areas where retrofit is indicated.

The units range from simple-to-use hand held scanners coupled with still cameras, to space-age video systems using high resolution video recording equipment. The less expensive units generally produce a black and white image, while the "state-of-the art" scanners analyze thermal radiation in a wide range of colors.

Whether in black and white or color, the pictures are simply measurements of radiation or reflected energy of the structure being viewed in rela-

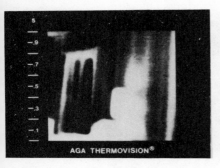

Uninsulated stud wall from inside. Cavity is darker (colder) than adjoining lighter (warmer) studs. Compare after insulation in picture at right.

After insulation is applied, cavity is warmer than studs and therefore appears lighter. Note how lit table lamp and window drapes affect scan.

tion to its temperature. Black and white pictures are interpreted with black being the cooler area and white the warmer.

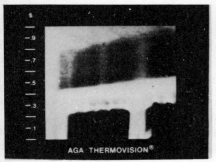

Almost as much cold penetrates uninsulated cavity between studs (dark grey) as through window (black).

After insulation is installed, filled wall cavity is an effective insulator (light grey). Dark studs are colder -relatively.

Generally, the most widely used color scanners show the hottest areas as red and the coolest as black.

Thermography units range in price from $500.00 to $40,000.00 plus. They can weigh as little as 7 pounds up to several hundred pounds.

But, it can still be cost effective as a tool for the average contractor or applicator. According to David McNally, Senior Vice-President, Standard Equipment Company of Milwaukee, Wisconsin, "The problem is that the large price tags and complicated operations associated with thermal imaging equipment have discouraged their wide spread use in industrial applications." He contends that most contractors using thermal imaging do so through service companies. "These companies," he adds, "have the equipment and the manpower for lease. But, for many people and many applications, this is by no means having equipment on site at all times."

Therefore, McNalley recommends purchase of what he describes as a "low cost, easy to use thermal imager." In this case, the Probeye™, manufactured by Hughs Aircraft Industrial Products Division.

Typical of the hand-held units is the Huges Probeye.®

Karl Reinke, President, Thermography of Illinois and Karl Reinke Co., Inc., of Dundee, Illinois holds just the opposite view "Don't invest in a small piece of equipment. They will eventually be technically outlawed. They're just not sensitive enough. You need an imaging system"

Reinke's company owns two of the most sophisticated systems available, the AGA Thermovision 750 and the Inframetric 610. Both units are in the $25,000.00 to $40,000.00 range.

Thermographic scans can be an excellent tool for checking insulation. It is a method of finding out how much insulation is missing and where. What it won't do is give the specific amounts of energy loss. A well trained operator can, however, give an estimate of the R-values for a wall.

The operator and/or the interpretation of information delivered by the scan is the most critical part of thermography. In the hands of an unqualified person, the best thermographic scan is all but useless. The operator should not only be trained in the use of current equipment but also be aware of advances in the field.

New and more sophisticated scanning devices are being introduced continually. It is recommended that before beginning a scan, the operator thoroughly examine the building. He should be aware of lamps and wall paintings as they will show up as variables on a sensitive scan or energy audit.

A new law is being introduced that would require an energy audit before a home is sold. At this time, it is unclear whether the legislation, when enacted, will apply to both new and old construction.

Additional government regulations are being prepared for infrared. ASRAE has standards for instrument use and ATSM has technical guides for operation. There are also new BEPS standards for new construction.

Thermography may be the "policeman" of insulations' future. As Reinke puts it, "If you don't put in what's specified, or what you say you're putting in, and apply the insulation in a qualitative manner you can -with infrared thermography -"be caught". A picture showing defects is hard to argue with successfully.

The average cost for a scan from a service will range from $.02 to $.12 per sq. ft. This could be just a visual examination of walls and suggestions for properly insulating or insulating repairs. More sophisticated scans which offer more data can run as high as $.20 per sq. ft.

Because of size, industrial scans are more expensive but may be cheaper if several buildings are examined together as might be the case in an industrial park.

A thorough scan should be done first on the outside, then on the inside of the structure for the best results. But, all buildings are not well suited for thermal imaging. Outer surfaces such as brick, stucco, and aluminum siding make it difficult to deliver an accurate scan. Metal, for example, will diffuse heat radically in all directions.

Weather and time are also major factors in infrared thermographic scanning.

Spring and Fall are the ideal seasons for weather, and dawn is the best time of the day for scanning. Second choice would be an overcast day which is cold and windless. Where exterior conditions don't allow accuracy, an interior scan of a vacated home is recommended (people and pets leave thermal "footprints"). The scan in this case will show cold air coming in as opposed to warm air going out.

Looking to the future, Jerry Hankins, Director, Quality Assurance, Scientific Applications, Inc., Mt. Pleasant, Iowa, feels that field measurement of the thermal value of a wall will be possible. "If the manufacturer of the insulation says the R-value of the insulation is such and such, you should be able to see it with a reasonable degree of accuracy. Thermography is the key to being able to show the customer he did get the thermal value he paid for."

ACKNOWLEDGEMENTS

Thanks and acknowledgements to the following for their assistance and cooperation:

John F. Weir, Public Communications Inc., St. Petersburg, Fla., 33702

The Celotex Corporation, Building Products Division, Raymond L. Delaney, Tampa, Fla., 33607

Dow Chemical U.S.A., Granville Research and Development Center, Granville, OH 43023

The Upjohn Company, CPR Division, George Bir, Torrance, CA 90503

Perlite Institute, Bill Hall, Director, Public Relations, N.Y., N.Y.

Vermiculite Assoc., John Cody, Technical Director, Atlanta, GA.

Mineral Insulation Manufacturer's Assoc., Inc., Sheldon Cady, Summit, N.J. 07901

Cellular Product Services, Inc., Phil McClain/Julie Canfield, Colorado Springs, CO 80907

Wilkin Insulation, Randy Wilkin, Jr., Mt. Prospect, Ill. 60056

Spray Insulation, Inc., John Gallagher, Skokie, Ill. 60007

BASF Wyandotte Corporation, Bill Fairweather, Wyandotte, MI 48192

Standard Equipment Co., Dave McNally, Milwaukee, WI 53224

Thermography of Illinois, Inc., Karl Reinke, Jr., Dundee, Ill. 60118

Ken MacCowan Co., Ken MacCowan, Glenview, Ill. 60025

Paul McShane, Arlington Heights, Ill.

Scientific Applications Inc., Denny Carlson, Jerry Hankins, Carl Frank, Mt. Pleasant, IA 52641

Southeastern Foam Products, Fred Reinhardt, Conyers, GA 30207

Johns-Manville Corporation, Bob Snow, Denver, CO 80217

Florida Energy Extension Service

North Dakota Energy Extension Service

Residential Conservation Service

U.S. Navy

MENSURATION

The information on the following pages will enable contractors and estimators to estimate quantities and costs accurately and in a minimum of time.

In a number of tables, the quantities are stated in decimals, as by using decimals, it is possible to state the fractional parts of inches, feet and yards, in a smaller space than where regular fractions are used.

For the contractor or estimator who is not thoroughly familiar with the decimal system, complete explanations are given covering the use of all classes of decimal fractions, so they may be used rapidly and accurately.

Estimating is nearly all "figures" of one kind or another, so it is essential that the contractor and estimator possess a fair working knowledge of arithmetic, if his estimates are to be accurate and dependable.

Most of the estimator's computations involve measurements of surface and cubical contents and are stated in lineal feet (lin.ft.), square feet (sq.ft.), square yards (sq.yds.), squares (sqs.) containing 100 sq. ft., cubic feet (cu.ft.), and cubic yards (cu.yds.). These quantities are often further reduced to thousands of brick, feet of lumber, board measure (b.m.), etc.

The rules on the following pages will enable the user to compute areas in square feet or cubical contents easily, accurately and quickly.

The following abbreviations are used throughout the book to make all tables brief and concise and to insert them in the smallest possible space :

	Abbreviation	Symbols
Inches	= in.	= "
Lineal feet	= lin. ft.	= '
Feet and inches	= ft. in.	= 2'-5"
Square feet	= sq. ft.	= □'
Square yards	= sq. yds.	= □yds.
Squares	= sqs.	
Cubic feet	= cu. ft.	
Cubic yards	= cu. yds.	
Board measure	= b. m.	

Linear Measure

12	inches	=12	in.=	12"	=1 foot	=1 ft.	=1'-0"
3	feet	= 3	ft.=	3'- 0"	=1 yard	=1 yd.	
16½	feet	=16½	ft.=	16'- 6"	=1 rod	=1 rd.	
40	rods	=40 rds.			=1 furlong	=1 fur.	
8	furlongs	= 8 fur.			=1 mile	=1 mi.	
5,280	feet	=1,760 yds.			=1 mile	=1 mi.	

Square Measure or Measures of Surfaces

144	square inches	= 144 sq. in.	= 1 square foot = 1 sq. ft.
9	square feet	= 9 sq. ft.	= 1 square yard = 1 sq. yd.
100	square feet	= 100 sq. ft.	= 1 square = 1 sq. (Architects' and Builders' Measure.)
30¼	square yards	= 30¼ sq. yds.	= 30.25 sq. yds. = 1 square rod = 1 sq. rd.
160	square rods	= 160 sq. rds.	= 1 Acre = 1 A.
43,560	sq. ft.	= 4,840 sq. yds.	= 1 Acre = 1 A.
640	acres	= 640 A.	= 1 square mile = 1 sq. mi.

Cubic Measure or Cubical Contents

1,728 cubic inches	=	1,728	cu. in.	= 1 cubic foot = 1 cu. Ft.
27 cubic feet	=	27	cu. ft.	= 1 cubic yard = 1 cu. yd.
128 cubic feet	=	128	cu. ft.	= 1 cord = 1 cd.
24¾ cubic feet	=	24¾	cu.ft.	= 24¾ cu. ft. =24.75 cu. ft. = 1 perch* = 1P.

*A perch of stone is nominally 16½ ft. long, 1 ft. high and 1½ ft. thick, and contains 24¾ cu. ft. However, in some states, especially west of the Mississippi, rubble work is figured by the perch containing 16½ cu. ft. Before submitting prices on masonry by the perch, find out the common practice in your locality.

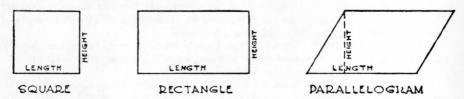

To Compute the Area of a Square, Rectangle or Parallelogram.—Multiply the length by the breadth or height. Example : Obtain the area of a wall 22 ft. (22'-0") long and 9 ft. (9'-0") high. 22x9=198 sq. ft.

To Compute the Area of a Triangle.—Multiply the base by ½ the altitude or perpendicular height. Example : Find the area of the end gable of a house 24 ft. (24'-0") wide and 12 ft. (12'-0") high from the base to high point of roof. 24 ft. x 6 ft. (½ the height)=144 sq. ft.

To Compute the Circumference of a Circle.—Multiply the diameter by 3.1416. The diameter multiplied by $3_{1/7}$ is close enough for all practical purposes. Example : Find the circumference or distance around a circle, the diameter of which is 12 ft. (12'-0"). 12x3.1416=37.6992 ft. the distance around the circle or 12x$3_{1/7}$=37.714 ft.

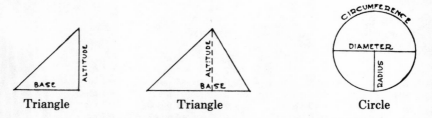

Triangle   Triangle   Circle

To Compute the Area of a Circle.—Multiply the square of the diameter by 0.7854 or multiply the square of the radius by 3.1416. Example : Find the area of a round concrete column 24 in. (24" or 2'-0") in diameter. The square of the diameter is 2x2=4.   4x0.7854=3.1416 sq. ft. the area of the circle.

The radius is ½ the diameter. If the diameter is 2 ft. (2'-0") the radius would be 1 ft. (1'-0"). To obtain the square of the radius, 1x1=1. Multiply the square of the radius, 1x3.1416=3.1416, the area of the circle.

To Compute the Cubical Contents of a Circular Column.—Multiply the area of the circle by the height. Example : Find the cubical contents of a round concrete column 2 ft. (2'-0") in diameter and 14 ft. (14'-0") long.

From the previous example, the area of a circle 2 ft. in diameter is 3.1416 sq. ft. 3.1416x14 ft. (the height)=43.9824 cu. ft. or for all practical purposes 44 cu. ft. of concrete in each column.

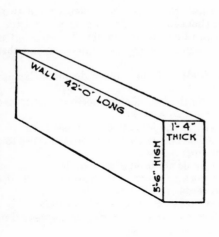

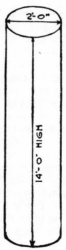

To Compute the Cubical Contents of any Solid. —Multiply the length by the breadth or height by the thickness. Computations of this kind are used extensively in estimating all classes of building work, such as excavating, concrete foundations, reinforced concrete, brick masonry, cut stone, granite, etc.

Example : Find the cubical contents of a wall 42 ft. (42'-0") long, 5 ft. 6 in. (5'-6") high, and 1 ft. 4 in. (1'-4") thick, 42'-0"x5'-6"x1'-4"=308 cu. ft. To reduce cu. ft. to cu. yds. divide 308 by 27, and the result is 11$\frac{11}{27}$ or 11½ or 11.41 cu. yds.

How to Use the Decimal System of Numerals in Estimating.—In construction work nearly all figures are either feet and inches or dollars and cents but inasmuch as it is convenient to use the decimal system in making many computations, a brief description of this system is given for the use of contractors and estimators who are not familiar with it.

A decimal is a fraction whose denominator is not written, but is some power of 10. They are often called decimal fractions but more often simply a decimal.

Example: We know 50 cents is 50/100 or 1/2 of a dollar. Writing the same thing in decimals would be $0.50.

Numerator	50
Denominator	100

When written as .50 or .5, it is a fraction whose denominator is not written, it being understood to be 10 from the fact that 5 occupies the first place to the right of the decimal point.

Therefore we have the following :

0.5	means 5/10, for the	5 extends to the	10th's place;
0.25	means 25/100 , for the	25 extends to the	100dth's place;
0.125	means 125/1000, for the	125 extends to the	1000dth's place.

The names of the places are, in part, as follows :

Thousands	Hundreds	Tens	Units	(Decimal Point)	Tenths	Hundredths	Thousands	Ten-Thousandths
1	3	4	5	.	2	7	6	5

This number is read "one thousand three hundred forty-five and two thousand seven hundred and sixty-five ten thousandths." The orders beyond the ten thousandths are hundred thousandths, millionths, ten millionths, etc., but in figuring construction work it is seldom necessary to carry the figures beyond three or four decimal points.

A whole number and a decimal together, form a mixed decimal. Example : 2.25 is the same as 2 25/100 or 2 1/4 .

The period written at the left of tenths is called the decimal point. Example. 0.5 = 5/10;   0.25 = 25/100 = 1/4 ;   0.375 = 375/1000 = 3/8, etc.

It is not necessary to write a zero at the left of the decimal point in the above examples, for 0.5 means the same as .5. The zero is often written there to call attention more quickly to the decimal point.

In the construction business, decimals are used chiefly to denote feet and inches, hours and minutes, the fractional working units of the various kinds of materials, and in money, which is dollars and cents or fractional parts of 100.

Table of Feet and Inches Reduced to Decimals

The following table illustrates how feet and inches may be expressed in four different ways, all meaning the same thing.

1	inch = 1	" = 1/12th	foot = 0.083
1 1/2	inches = 1 1/2"	= 1/8th	foot = 0.125
2	inches = 2	" = 1/6th	foot = 0.1667
2 1/2	inches = 2 1/2"	= 5/24ths	foot = 0.2087
3	inches = 3	" = 1/4th	foot = 0.25
3 1/2	inches = 3 1/2"	= 7/24ths	foot = 0.2917
4	inches = 4	" = 1/3rd	foot = 0.333
4 1/2	inches = 4 1/2"	= 3/8ths	foot = 0.375
5	inches = 5	" = 5/12ths	foot = 0.417
5 1/2	inches = 5 1/2"	= 11/24ths	foot = 0.458
6	inches = 6	" = 1/2	foot = 0.5
6 1/2	inches = 6 1/2"	= 13/24ths	foot = 0.5417
7	inches = 7	" = 7/12ths	foot = 0.583
7 1/2	inches = 7 1/2"	= 5/8ths	foot = 0.625
8	inches = 8	" = 2/3rds	foot = 0.667
8 1/2	inches = 8 1/2"	= 17/24ths	foot = 0.708
9	inches = 9	" = 3/4ths	foot = 0.75
9 1/2	inches = 9 1/2"	= 19/24ths	foot = 0.792
10	inches = 10	" = 5/6ths	foot = 0.833
10 1/2	inches = 10 1/2"	= 7/8ths	foot = 0.875
11	inches = 11	" = 11/12ths	foot = 0.917
11 1/2	inches = 11 1/2"	= 23/24ths	foot = 0.958
12	inches = 12	" = 1	foot = 1.0

Example : Write 5 feet, 7 1/2 inches, in decimals. It would be written 5.625, Which is equivalent to 5 5/8 feet.

Table of Common Fractions Stated in Decimals

The following table gives the decimal equivalents of common fractions frequently used in estimating :

$$1/16 = \frac{6 1/4}{100} = 0.0625 \qquad 7/16 = \frac{43 3/4}{100} = 0.4375$$

$$1/8 = \frac{12 1/2}{100} = 0.125 \qquad 1/2 = \frac{50}{100} = 0.5$$

$$3/16 = \frac{18 3/4}{100} \quad 0.1875 \qquad 9/16 = \frac{56 1/4}{100} = 0.5625$$

Table of Common Fractions Stated in Decimals—Cont'd.

$$1/4 = \frac{25}{100} = 0.25$$

$$5/8 = \frac{62\,1/2}{100} = 0.625$$

$$5/16 = \frac{31\,1/4}{100} = 0.3125$$

$$11/16 = \frac{68\,3/4}{100} = 0.6875$$

$$3/8 = \frac{37\,1/2}{100} = 0.375$$

$$3/4 = \frac{75}{100} = 0.75$$

$$13/16 = \frac{81\,1/4}{100} = 0.8125$$

$$15/16 = \frac{93\,3/4}{100} = 0.9375$$

$$7/8 = \frac{87\,1/2}{100} = 0.875$$

$$8/8 = \frac{100}{100} = 1.0$$

Annexing zeros to a number does not change its value; 0.5 is the same as 0.500.

Table of Hours and Minutes Reduced to Decimals

The following table illustrates how minutes may be reduced to fractional parts of hours and to decimal parts of hours.

Number of Minutes		Fractional Part of an Hour		Decimal Part of an Hour	Number of Minutes		Fractional Part of an Hour		Decimal Part of an Hour
1	=	1/60th	=	0.0167	31	=	31/60ths	=	0.5167
2	=	1/30th	=	0.0333	32	=	8/15ths	=	0.5333
3	=	1/20th	=	0.05	33	=	11/20ths	=	0.55
4	=	1/15th	=	0.0667	34	=	17/30ths	=	0.5667
5	=	1/12th	=	0.0833	35	=	7/12ths	=	0.5833
6	=	1/10th	=	0.10	36	=	3/5ths	=	0.60
7	=	7/60ths	=	0.1167	37	=	37/60ths	=	0.6167
8	=	2/15ths	=	0.1333	38	=	19/30ths	=	0.6333
9	=	3/20ths	=	0.15	39	=	13/20ths	=	0.65
10	=	1/6th	=	0.1667	40	=	2/3rds	=	0.6667
11	=	11/60ths	=	0.1833	41	=	41/60ths	=	0.6833
12	=	1/5th	=	0.20	42	=	7/10ths	=	0.70
13	=	13/60ths	=	0.2167	43	=	43/60ths	=	0.7167
14	=	7/30ths	=	0.2333	44	=	11/15ths	=	0.7333
15	=	1/4th	=	0.25	45	=	3/4ths	=	0.75
16	=	4/15ths	=	0.2667	46	=	23/30ths	=	0.7667
17	=	17/60ths	=	0.2833	47	=	47/60ths	=	0.7833
18	=	3/10ths	=	0.30	48	=	4/5ths	=	0.80
19	=	19/60ths	=	0.3167	49	=	49/60ths	=	0.8167
20	=	1/3rd	=	0.333	50	=	5/6ths	=	0.8333
21	=	7/20ths	=	0.35	51	=	51/60ths	=	0.85
22	=	11/30ths	=	0.3667	52	=	13/15ths	=	0.8667
23	=	23/60ths	=	0.3833	53	=	53/60ths	=	0.8833
24	=	2/5ths	=	0.40	54	=	9/10ths	=	0.90
25	=	5/12ths	=	0.4167	55	=	11/12ths	=	0.9167
26	=	13/30ths	=	0.4333	56	=	14/15ths	=	0.9333
27	=	9/20ths	=	0.45	57	=	19/20ths	=	0.95
28	=	7/15ths	=	0.4667	58	=	29/30ths	=	0.9667
29	=	29/60ths	=	0.4833	59	=	59/60ths	=	0.9833
30	=	1/2	=	0.5	60	=	1	=	1.0

Example: Write 4 hours and 37 minutes in decimals. It would be written 4.6167.

Now find the labor cost for 4.6167 hrs. at $7.50 an hr.

```
            Hours,        4.6167
      X Hourly Rate,      $7.50
                        2308350
                        323169
      Total Cost,  $34.625250  or $34.63
```

Similar Decimals.—Decimals that have the same number of decimal places are called similar decimals. Thus, 0.75 and 0.25 are similar decimals and so are 0.150 and 0.275; but 0.15 and 0.275 are dissimilar decimals.

To reduce dissimilar decimals to similar decimals, give them the same number of decimal places by annexing or cutting off zeros. Example, 0.125, 0.25, 0.375 and 0.5 may all be reduced to thousandths as follows : 0.125, 0.250, 0.375 and 0.500.

To Reduce a Decimal to a Common Fraction.—Omit the decimal point, write the denominator of the decimal, and then reduce the common fraction to its lowest terms.

Example : 0.375 equals 375/1000, which reduced to its lowest terms, equals 3/8.

$$25 \left| \frac{375}{1000} \right. = 5 \left| \frac{15}{40} \right. = \text{\textthreeeighths}$$

How to Add Decimals.—To add numbers containing decimals, write like orders under one another, and then add as with whole numbers. Example, add 0.125, 0.25, 0.375, and 1.0.

The total of the addition is 1.750, which equals 1 750/1000, and which may be further reduced to 13/4

```
0.125
0.25
0.375
1.0
1.750
```

How to Subtract Decimals.—To subtract one number from another, when either or both contain decimals, reduce to similar decimals, write like orders under one another, and subtract as with whole numbers.

Subtract 20 hours and 37 minutes from 27 hours and 13 minutes, both being written in decimals, The difference is 6.6000 or 6.6 hours, which reduced to a common fraction is 63/5 hours or 6 hours and 36 minutes.

```
27.2167
20.6167
6.6000
```

How to Multiply Decimals.—The same method is used as in multiplying other numbers, and the result should contain as many decimal points as there are in both of the numbers multiplied.

Example: Multiply 3 feet by 6 inches by 4 feet 9 inches

4 ft. 9 in.=4'-9"=4¾ ft.=4.75 Mutiplicand
3 ft. 6 in.=3'-6"=3½ ft.=3.5 Multiplier
To multiply, proceed as illustrated

```
        4.75
        3.5
       2375
       1425
Product  16625 or 16.625
```

In the above example, there are 2 decimals in the multiplicand and 1 decimal in the multiplier. The result or product should contain the same number of decimals as the multiplicand and multiplier combined, which is three. Starting at the right and counting to the left three places, place the decimal point between the two sixes The result would be 16.625, which equals 16 625/1000= 16 5/8 sq. ft.

Practical Examples Using Decimals

The quantities of cement, sand and gravel required for one cu. yd. of concrete are ordinarily stated in decimals. For instance, a cu. yd. of concrete mixed in the proportions of 1 part cement ; 2 parts sand ; and 4 parts gravel, is usually stated 1: 2 : 4 and requires the following materials :

1.50 bbls. cement = 150/100 bbls. = 1½ bbls. = 6 sacks.
0.42 cu. yds. sand = 42/100 cu. yds. = 21/50 cu. yds. = 11 1/3 cu. ft.
0.84 cu. yds. gravel = 84/100 cu. yds. = 22 2/3 cu. ft.

There are 4 sacks of cement to the bbl., and each sack weighs 94 lbs. and contains approximately 1 cu. ft. of cement.

There are 27 cu. ft. in a cu. yd.; to obtain the number of cu. ft. of sand required for a yard of concrete, 0.42 cu. yds = 42/100 cu. yds. = 21/50 cu. yds. and 21/50 of 27

$$\text{cu. ft.} = \frac{21 \times 27}{50} = \frac{567}{50} \quad .567 \div 50 = 11.34 \text{ or } 11\frac{1}{3} \text{ cu. ft. sand.}$$

To find the cost of a cu. yd. of concrete based on the above quantities, and assuming it requires 2¼ hrs. labor time to mix and place one cu. yd. of concrete, proceed as follows :

1½ bbls. cement	= 1.50 bbls. cement @	$9.00 per bbl. =	$13.5000
11 1/3 cu. ft. sand	= 0.42 cu. yd. sand @	5.75 per cu. yd. =	2.4150
22 2/3 cu. ft. gravel	= 0.84 cu. yd. gravel @	5.75 per cu. yd. =	4.8300
2¼ hrs. labor	= 2.25 hrs. labor @	9.80 per hr. =	22.0500
	Cost per cu. yd.		$42.7950

You will note the total is carried in four decimal places. This is to illustrate the actual figures obtained by multiplying. The total would be $42.80 per cu. yd. of concrete.

In making the above multiplications you will note there are 2 decimals in both the multiplicand and the multiplier of all the amounts multiplied, so the result should contain as many decimals as the sum of the multiplicand and multiplier, which is 4. You will note all the totals contain 4 decimal places. Always bear this in mind when making your multiplications because if the decimal place is wrong it makes a difference of 90 percent in your total. You know the correct result is $42.7950 but suppose by mistake you counted off 5 decimal places. The result would be $4.27950 or $4.28 per cu. yd. or just about 1/10 enough; or if you made a mistake the other way and counted off just 3 decimal places, the result would be $427.950 or $427.95 per cu. yd., or just about 10 times too much. Watch your decimal places.

The same method is used in estimating lumber. All kinds of framing lumber are ordinarily sold by the 1,000 ft., b.m., so 1,000 is the unit or decimal used when estimating lumber.

Suppose you buy 150 pcs. of 2"x8"-16'-0", which contains 3,200 ft. b.m. This is equivalent to 3200/1000 = 32/10 = 3 1/5 thousandths or stated in decimals it may be either 3.2 or 3.200. The cost of this lumber at $230.00 per 1,000 ft. b.m., would be obtained by multiplying 3.200 ft. at $230.00 per 1,000 ft. b. m., as follows :
3.200 M ft. of lumber @ $736.00000 or $736.00.

Note there were 3 decimal places in the multiplicand and 2 decimal places in the multiplier, so the result should contain 5 decimal places, but inasmuch as all the decimals are zeros, drop all but two of them to designate 736 dollars and no cents.

Things to Remember When Using Decimals

.	at the left of a figure indicates a decimal.
.6	indicates tenths, thus .6 = 6/10 = .60 = 60/100 = .600 = 600/1000
.06	indicates hundredths, thus .06 = 6/100 = .060 = 60/1000
.006	indicates thousandths, thus .006 = 6/1000
.0006	indicates ten thousandths, thus .0006 = 6/10000

When multiplying decimals always remember that the result or product must contain as many decimal places as the sum of the decimal places in both the multiplicand and the multiplier ; thus : Find the cost of 3 hrs. 20 min. laborer's time at $9.80 an hr.

3 hrs. 20 min. equal 3/⅓ hrs.　　　　　=3.3333 Multiplicand
7 dollars 50 cents an hr.　　　　　　　= 　9.80 Multiplier

There are 3 decimals in the multiplicand　　2666640
and 2 decimals in the multiplier, so the re-　299997
sult or total should contain as many decimals　32666340=32.666340=$32.67
as the sum of the multiplicand and multi-
plier, which is 5.

Be sure your decimal point is in the RIGHT place and the rest is easy.

Conversion Factors
S. I. Metric - English Systems

Multiply	by	to obtain
acres	0.404687	hectares
"	4.04687×10^{-3}	square kilometers
ares	1076.39	square feet
board feet	144 sq in. X 1 in.	cubic inches
"　"	0.0833	cubic feet
bushels	0.3521	hectoliters
centimeters	3.28083×10^{-2}	feet
"	0.3937	inches
cubic centimeters	3.53145×10^{-5}	cubic feet
"　"	6.102×10^{-2}	cubic inches
cubic feet	2.8317×10^4	cubic centimeters
"　"	2.8317×10^{-2}	cubic meters
"　"	6.22905	gallons, Imperial
"　"	0.2832	hectoliters
"　"	28.3170	liters
"　"	2.38095×10^{-2}	tons, British shipping
"　"	0.025	tons, U.S. shipping
cubic inches	16.38716	cubic centimeters
cubic meters	35.3145	cubic feet
"　"	1.30794	cubic yards
"　"	264.2	gallons, U. S.
cubic yards	0.764559	cubic meters
"　"	7.6336	hectoliters
degrees, angular	0.0174533	radians
degrees, F (less 32 F)	0.5556	degrees, C
"　C	1.8	degrees, F (less 32 F)
foot pounds	0.13826	kilogram meters
feet	30.4801	centimeters
"	0.304801	meters
"	304.801	millimeters
"	1.64468×10^{-4}	miles, nautical
gallons, Imperial	0.160538	cubic feet
"　"	1.20091	gallons, U. S.
"　"	4.54596	liters
gallons, U.S	0.832702	gallons, Imperial
"　"	0.13368	cubic feet
"　"	231.	cubic inches
"　"	0.0378	hectoliters
"　"	3.78543	liters
grams, metric	2.20462×10^{-3}	pounds, avoirdupois
hectares	2.47104	acres
"	1.076387×10^5	square feet

Conversion Factors (Cont'd)

Multiply	by	to obtain
hectares	3.86101×10^{-3}	square miles
hectoliters	3.531	cubic feet
"	2.84	bushels
"	0.131	cubic yards
hectoliters	26.42	gallons
horsepower, metric	0.98632	horsepower, U. S.
horsepower, U.S.	1.01387	horsepower, metric
inches	2.54001	centimeters
"	2.54001×10^{-2}	meters
"	25.4001	millimeters
kilograms	2.20462	pounds
"	9.84206×10^{-4}	long tons
"	1.10231×10^{-3}	short tons
kilogram meters	7.233	foot pounds
kilograms per m	0.671972	pounds per ft
kilograms per sq cm	14.2234	pounds per sq in.
kilograms per sq m	0.204817	pounds per sq ft
" " " "	9.14362×10^{-5}	long tons per sq ft
kilograms per sq mm	1422.34	pounds per sq in.
" " " "	0.634973	long tons per sq. in.
kilograms per cu m	6.24283×10^{-2}	pounds per cu ft
kilometers	0.62137	miles, statute
"	0.53959	miles, nautical
"	3280.7	feet
liters	0.219975	gallons, Imperial
"	0.26417	gallons, U.S.
"	3.53145×10^{-2}	cubic feet
"	61.022	cubic inches
meters	3.28083	feet
"	39.37	inches
"	1.09361	yards
miles, statute	1.60935	kilometers
" "	0.8684	miles, nautical
miles, nautical	6080.204	feet
· " "	1.85325	kilometers
" "	1.1516	miles, statute
millimeters	3.28083×10^{-3}	feet
"	3.937×10^{-2}	inches
pounds, avoirdupois	453.592	grams, metric
" "	0.453592	kilograms
" "	4.464×10^{-4}	tons, long
" "	4.53592×10^{-4}	tons, metric
pounds per ft	1.48816	kilograms per m

Conversion Factors (Cont'd)

Multiply	by	to obtain
pounds per sq ft..............	4.88241	kilograms per sq m
pounds per sq in..............	7.031×10^{-2}	kilograms per sq cm
" " " "	7.031×10^{-4}	kilograms per sq mm
pounds per cu ft..............	16.0184	kilograms per cu m
radians............................	57.29578	degrees, angular
square centimeters..........	0.1550	square inches
square feet.......................	9.29034×10^{-4}	ares
square feet.......................	9.29034×10^{-6}	hectares
" "	0.0929034	square meters
square inches...................	6.45163	square centimeters
" "	645.163	square millimeters
square kilometers.............	247.104	acres
" "	0.3861	square miles
square meters..................	10.7639	square feet
" "	1.19599	square yards
square miles.....................	259.0	hectares
" "	2.590	square kilometers
square millimeters...........	1.550×10^{-3}	square inches
square yards....................	0.83613	square meters
tons, long...........................	1016.05	kilograms
" "	2240.	pounds
" "	1.01605	tons, metric
" "	1.120	tons, short
tons, long, per sq ft.........	1.09366×10^{-4}	kilograms per sq m
tons, long, per sq in........	1.57494	kilograms per sq mm
tons, metric......................	2204.62	pounds
" "	0.98421	tons, long
" "	1.10231	tons, short
tons, short	907.185	kilograms
" "	0.892857	tons, long
" "	0.907185	tons, metric
tons, British shipping......	42.00	cubic feet
" " "	0.952381	tons, U. S. shipping
tons, U. S. shipping.........	40.00	cubic feet
" " "	1.050	tons, British shipping
yards..............................	0.914402	meters

GENERAL BUILDING INSULATION COMPARISON CHART

GENERIC BUILDING INSULATION COMPARISON CHART
(Adapted from U.S. Navy's "Building Insulation Material Compilation", 1980)

Generic Insulation	R/inch	K (approx)	lb/ft3	Approx. Cost Installed (¢ per S.F.)	Advantages	Disadvantages	Federal Spec. and/or ASTM Standard
BATTS & BLANKETS							
Fiber Glass	3.2	0.32	0.6-1.0	3.5-4.5	Low cost, non-combustible w/o facings, stable.	Facings may be combustible, binders may burn out.	HH-I-521E/C553-70/ C262-64 (76)
Rock Wool	3.6-3.7	0.27-0.28	1.5-2.5	3.5-5.5	Low cost, non-combustible w/o facings, stable.	Facings may be combustible, binders may burn out.	HH-I-521E/C553-70/ C262-64 (76)
BOARDS							
Cellular Glass	2.63	0.38	8.5	10.0-14.0*	High compressive strength, non-combustible, impermeable to moisture, stable.	High cost, low R per inch, possible freeze-thaw damage when in contact with water.	HH-I-551E/C552
Mineral Fiber with Binder	3.45	0.29	15	5.0-7.5	Provides structural support, fire resistant, stable.	Moderate cost. Modest R per inch. Binder may be combustible.	HH-I-55B/C612-70/ C726-72
Polyurethane & polyisocyanurate foam	unfaced: 6.2-5.8 faced: 7.1-7.7	unfaced: 0.16-.17 faced: 0.13-.14	2.0	3.0-6.5	High R per inch, may provide infiltration seal, low moisture absorption, stable.	Moderate cost, combustible (Polyisocyanurate is less so than polyurethane), non-structural.	HH-I-530A/C591-69
Fiber Glass	4.25	0.24	3.0	8.0-14.0*	Good R per inch, low combustibility, good accoustical absorption, stable.	High cost, binders may burn out.	MIL-I-742
Expanded Polystyrene foam	extruded 5.0 molded: 3.9-4.4	extruded 0.20 molded: 0.23-.26	0.8-3.0	3.0-5.5	Good R per inch, may provide infiltration seal, low moisture absorption, stable.	Combustible, nonstructural.	HH-I-524B/ MIL-P40619/ MIL-P-43110/ CE-204/C-578-69
Perlite	2.8	0.36	11.0	-	Low combustibility, stable.	Low R per inch.	C-728
Mineral Fiber with foam	3.7-7.3	0.14-.27	NA	4.0-6.5	Mineral board acts as a fire barrier to protect foam. Can provide structural support, stable.	Foam is combustible.	-
Wood Fiber	2.1-2.4	0.42-47	25	4.0-6.5	Availability, can provide structural support, stable.	Combustible.	C208-72/C532
Insulating Concrete	0.8-2.0	0.50-1.17	20-40	-	Non-combustible, can provide structural support, stable.	Low R per inch.	C196-61

* Materials only

GENERIC BUILDING INSULATION COMPARISON CHART (Concluded)

Generic Insulation	$\frac{R}{Inch}$	K (approx)	$\frac{lb}{ft^3}$	Approx. Cost Installed (¢ per S.F.)	Advantages	Disadvantages	Federal Specs. and/or ASTM Standard
LOOSE FILL							
Cellulose	3.2-3.7	0.27-0.31	2.2-3.0	Poured: 1.5-3.0 Blown: 3.5-6.0 Sprayed: 11.0-20.0	Low cost, good R per inch, availability.	High moisture permeability and some absorption, may settle 0-20% if installed at too low a density.	HH-I-515D C0739-73
Fiber Glass	2.2	0.45	0.6-1.0	Blown:4.0-6.5	Low cost, non-combustible.	Low R per inch, high moisture permeability, may settle.	HH-I-103A C764-73
Rock Wool	2.9	0.34	1.5-2.5	Blown: 4.0-6.5	Low cost, non-combustible.	Modest R per inch, high moisture permeability, may settle.	HH-I-1030A C764-73
Perlite	2.5-3.7	0.27-0.40	2-11	-	Low cost, non-combustible, stable.	High moisture permeability.	HH-I-574B C549-73
Vermiculite	2.4-3.0	0.33-0.41	4-10	-	Low cost, non-combustible, stable.	High moisture permeability.	HH-I-585 C516-75
FOAM IN PLACE							
Polyurethane/polyisocyanurate	5.8-6.2	0.16-0.17	2.0	-	High R per inch, may provide infiltration seal, low moisture absorption.	Moderate cost, combustible (polyisocyanurate is less so than polyurethane). May experience some shrinkage.	
Urea-based mixtures	4.2	0.23	0.6-0.9	4.5-6.5	High R per inch, may provide infiltration seal.	Moderate cost, combustible, improperly installed foam may shrink significantly and/or cause lingering formaldehyde vapors.	
REFLECTIVE INSULATION							
2 Layer 3 Layer	R-5 R-7.5	-	-	1.5-4.0	Low cost, non-combustible, can provide infiltration seal, low thermal mass.	Poor performance where conduction or convection dominate, dust on reflective surfaces may reduce performance.	HH-I-1252B C-236

Appendix B

INSULATING VALUES OF CONSTRUCTION MATERIALS

Insulating Values of Construction Materials

1. Conductivities (k), Conductances (C) and Resistances (R) of Building and Insulating Materials

(The constants are expressed in Btu/hr·sq ft·°F. Conductivities are per inch thickness, and Conductances are for thickness or construction stated, but not per inch thickness. All values are for a mean temperature of 75°F, except as noted by an (*) which have been reported at 45°F.)

Description		Density (lb/ft³)	Conductivity (k)	Conductance (C)	Per inch thickness (1/k)	Resistance¹ (R) For thickness listed (1/C)	Specific Heat, Btu/(lb)(deg F)
Building Board							
Boards, Panels, Subflooring, Sheathing, Woodboard Panel Products							
Asbestos-cement board		120	4.00	—	0.25	—	0.24
Asbestos-cement board	0.125 in	120	—	33.00	—	0.03	
Asbestos-cement board	0.25 in	120	—	16.50	—	0.06	
Gypsum or plaster board	0.375 in	50	—	3.10	—	0.32	0.26
Gypsum or plaster board	0.5 in	50	—	2.22	—	0.45	
Gypsum or plaster board	0.625 in	50	—	1.78	—	0.56	
Plywood (Douglas fir)		34	0.80	—	1.25	—	0.29
Plywood (Douglas fir)	0.25 in	34	—	3.20	—	0.31	
Plywood (Douglas fir)	0.375 in	34	—	2.13	—	0.47	
Plywood (Douglas fir)	0.5 in	34	—	1.60	—	0.62	
Plywood (Douglas fir)	0.625 in	34	—	1.29	—	0.77	
Plywood or wood panels	0.75 in	34	—	1.07	—	0.93	0.29
Vegetable fiber board							
Sheathing, regular density	0.5 in	18	—	0.76	—	1.32	0.31
	0.78125 in	18	—	0.49	—	2.06	
Sheathing, intermediate density	0.5 in	22	—	0.82	—	1.22	0.31
Nail-base sheathing	0.5 in	25	—	0.88	—	1.14	0.31
Shingle backer	0.375 in	18	—	1.06	—	0.94	0.31
Shingle backer	0.3125 in	18	—	1.28	—	0.78	
Sound deadening board	0.5 in	15	—	0.74	—	1.35	0.30
Tile and lay-in panels, plain or acoustic	0.5 in	18	—	0.80	—	1.25	
	0.75 in	18	—	0.53	—	1.89	
Laminated paperboard		30	0.50	—	2.00	—	0.33
Homogeneous board from repulped paper		30	0.50	—	2.00	—	0.28
Hardboard							
Medium density		50	0.73	—	1.37	—	0.31
High density, service temp. service underlay		55	0.82	—	1.22	—	0.32
High density, std. tempered		63	1.00	—	1.00	—	0.32
Particleboard							
Low density		37	0.54	—	1.85	—	0.31
Medium density		50	0.94	—	1.06	—	0.31
High density		62.5	1.18	—	0.85	—	0.31
Underlayment	0.625 in	40	—	1.22	—	0.82	0.29
Wood subfloor	0.75 in		—	1.06	—	0.94	0.33
Building Membrane							
Vapor—permeable felt		—	—	16.70	—	0.06	
Vapor—seal, 2 layes of mopped 15-lb felt		—	—	8.35	—	0.12	
Vapor-seal, plastic film		—	—	—	—	Negl.	
Finish Flooring Materials							
Carpet and fibrous pad		—	—	0.48	—	2.08	0.34
Carpet and rubber pad		—	—	0.81	—	1.23	0.33
Cork tile	0.125 in	—	—	3.60	—	0.28	0.48
Terrazzo	1 in.	—	—	12.50	—	0.08	0.19
Tile—asphalt, linoleum, vinyl, rubber		—	—	20.00	—	0.05	0.30
vinyl asbestos							0.24
ceramic							0.19
Wood, hardwood finish	0.75 in.			1.47		0.68	
Insulating Materials							
Blanket and Batt							
Mineral fiber, fibrous form processed from							
rock, slag, or glass							
approx.¹ 2-2.75 in.		0.3-2.0	—	0.143	—	7	0.17-0.2
approx.¹ 3-3.5 in.		0.3-2.0	—	0.091	—	11	
approx.¹ 3.5-6.5 in.		0.3-2.0	—	0.053	—	19	
approx.¹ 6-7 in.		0.3-2.0	—	0.045	—	22	
approx.¹ 8.5 in.		0.3-2.0	—	0.033	—	30	

Description	Density (lb/ft³)	Conductivity (k)	Conductance (C)	Resistance¹ (R) Per inch thickness (1/k)	Resistance¹ (R) For thickness listed (1/C)	Specific Heat, Btu/(lb) (deg F)
Board and Slabs						
Cellular glass	8.5	0.38	—	2.63	—	0.24
Glass fiber, organic bonded	4-9	0.25	—	4.00	—	0.23
Expanded rubber (rigid)	4.5	0.22	—	4.55	—	0.40
Expanded polystyrene extruded Cut cell surface	1.8	0.25	—	4.00	—	0.29
Expanded polystyrene extruded Smooth skin surface	2.2	0.20	—	5.00	—	0.29
Expanded polystyrene extruded Smooth skin surface	3.5	0.19	—	5.26	—	
Expanded polystyrene, molded beads	1.0	0.28	—	3.57	—	0.29
Expanded polyurethane² (R-11 exp.)	1.5	0.16	—	6.25	—	0.38
(thickness 1 in. or greater)	2.5					
Mineral fiber with resin binder	15	0.29	—	3.45	—	0.17
Mineral fiberboard, wet felted Core or roof insulation	16-17	0.34	—	2.94	—	
Acoustical tile	18	0.35	—	2.86	—	0.19
Acoustical tile	21	0.37	—	2.70	—	
Mineral fiberboard, wet molded Acoustical tile²	23	0.42	—	2.38	—	0.14
Wood or cane fiberboard Acoustical tile² . . . . 0.5 in.	—	—	0.80	—	1.25	0.31
Acoustical tile . . . . 0.75 in.	—	—	0.53	—	1.89	
Interior finish (plank, tile)	15	0.35	—	2.86	—	0.32
Wood shredded (cemented in preformed slabs)	22	0.60	—	1.67	—	0.31
Loose Fill						
Cellulosic insulation (milled paper or wood pulp)	2.3-3.2	0.27-0.32	—	3.13-3.70	—	0.33
Sawdust or shavings	8.0-15.0	0.45	—	2.22	—	0.33
Wood fiber, softwoods	2.0-3.5	0.30	—	3.33	—	0.33
Perlite, expanded	5.0-8.0	0.37	—	2.70	—	0.26
Mineral fiber (rock, slag or glass) approx. 3.75-5 in.	0.6-2.0	—	—		11	0.17
approx. 6.5-8.75 in.	0.6-2.0	—	—		19	
approx. 7.5-10 in.	0.6-2.0	—	—		22	
approx. 10.25-13.75 in.	0.6-2.0	—	—		30	
Vermiculite, exfoliated	7.0-8.2	0.47	—	2.13	—	3.20
	4.0-6.0	0.44		2.27	—	
Roof Insulation⁴						
Preformed, for use above deck Different roof insulations are available in different thicknesses to provide the design C values listed. Consult individual manufacturers for actual thickness of their material.			0.72 to 0.12		1.39 to 8.33	
Masonry Materials						
Concretes						
Cement mortar	116	5.0	—	0.20	—	
Gypsum-fiber concrete 87.5% gypsum, 12.5% wood chips	51	1.66	—	0.60	—	0.21
Lightweight aggregates including expanded	120	5.2	—	0.19	—	
shale, clay, or slate; expanded	100	3.6	—	0.28	—	
slags; cinders; pumice; vermiculite;	80	2.5	—	0.40	—	
also cellular concretes	60	1.7	—	0.59	—	
	40	1.15	—	0.86	—	
	30	0.90	—	1.11	—	
	20	0.70		1.43		
Perlite, expanded	40	0.93		1.08		
	30	0.71		1.41		
	20	0.50		2.00		0.32
Sand and gravel or stone aggregate (oven dried)	140	9.0	—	0.11		0.22
Sand and gravel or stone aggregate (not dried)	140	12.0	—	0.08		
Stucco	116	5.0	—	0.20		
Masonry Units						
Brick, common²	120	5.0	—	0.20	—	0.19
Brick, face²	130	9.0	—	0.11	—	

| | | | | | Resistance[1] (R) | |
Description	Density (lb/ft[3])	Conductivity (k)	Conductance (C)	Per inch thickness (1/k)	For thickness listed (1/C)	Specific Heat, Btu/(lb) (deg F)
Masonry Units (continued)						
Clay tile, hollow:						
1 cell deep .... 3 in.	—	—	1.25	—	0.80	0.21
1 cell deep .... 4 in.	—	—	0.90	—	1.11	
2 cells deep .... 6 in.	—	—	0.66	—	1.52	
2 cells deep .... 8 in.	—	—	0.54	—	1.85	
2 cells deep .... 10 in.	—	—	0.45	—	2.22	
3 cells deep .... 12 in.	—	—	0.40	—	2.50	
Concrete blocks, three oval core:						
Sand and gravel aggregate .... 4 in.	—	—	1.40	—	0.71	0.22
.... 8 in.	—	—	0.90	—	1.11	
.... 12 in.	—	—	0.78	—	1.28	
Cinder aggregate .... 3 in.	—	—	1.16	—	0.86	0.21
.... 4 in.	—	—	0.90	—	1.11	
.... 8 in.	—	—	0.58	—	1.72	
.... 12 in.	—	—	0.53	—	1.89	
Lightweight aggregate .... 3 in.	—	—	0.79	—	1.27	0.21
(expanded shale, clay, slate .... 4 in.	—	—	0.67	—	1.50	
or slag; pumice) .... 8 in.	—	—	0.50	—	2.00	
.... 12 in.	—	—	0.44	—	2.27	
Concrete blocks, rectangular core**						
Sand and gravel aggregate						
2 core, 8 in. 36 lb.**	—	—	0.96	—	1.04	0.22
Same with filled cores**	—	—	0.52	—	1.93	0.22
Lightweight aggregate (expanded shale,						
clay, slate or slag, pumice):						
3 core, 6 in. 19 lb.**	—	—	0.61	—	1.65	0.21
Same with filled cores**'	—	—	0.33	—	2.99	
2 core, 8 in. 24 lb.**	—	—	0.46	—	2.18	
Same with filled cores**'	—	—	0.20	—	5.03	
3 core, 12 in. 38 lb.**	—	—	0.40	—	2.48	
Same with filled cores**'	—	—	0.17*	—	5.82	
Stone, lime or sand	—	12.50	—	0.08	—	0.19
Gypsum, partition tile:						
3 x 12 x 30 in. solid	—	—	0.79	—	1.26	0.19
3 x 12 x 30 in. 4-cell	--	—	0.74	—	1.35	
4 x 12 x 30 in. 3-cell	—	—	0.60	—	1.67	
Plastering Materials						
Cement plaster, sand aggregate	116	5.0	—	0.20	—	0.20
Sand aggretate .... 0.375 in.	—	—	13.33	—	0.08	0.20
Sand aggregate .... 0.75 in.	—	—	6.66	—	0.15	0.20
Gypsum plaster:						
Lightweight aggregate .... 0.5 in.	45	—	3.12	—	0.32	
Lightweight aggregate .... 0.625 in.	45	—	2.67	—	0.39	
Lightweight agg. on metal lath .... 0.75 in.	—	—	2.13	—	0.47	
Perlite aggregate	45	1.5	—	0.67	—	0.32
Sand aggregate	105	5.6	—	0.18	—	0.20
Sand aggregate .... 0.5 in.	105	—	11.10	—	0.09	
Sand aggregate .... 0.625 in.	105	—	9.10	—	0.11	
Sand aggregate on metal lath .... 0.75 in.	—	—	7.70	—	0.13	
Vermiculite aggregate	45	1.7	—	0.59	—	
Roofing						
Asbestos-cement shingles 120	—	4.76	—	0.21	0.24	
Asphalt roll roofing	70	—	6.50	—	0.15	0.36
Asphalt shingles	70	—	2.27	—	0.44	0.30
Built-up roofing .... 0.375 in.	70	—	3.00	—	0.33	0.35
Slate .... 0.5 in.	—	—	20.00	—	0.05	0.30
Wood shingles, plain and plastic film faced	—	—	1.06	—	0.94	0.31

Description	Density (lb/ft³)	Conductivity (k)	Conductance (C)	Per inch thickness (1/k)	Resistance (R) For thickness listed (1/C)	Specific Heat, Btu/lb (deg F)
Siding Materials (on Flat Surface)						
Shingles						
Asbestos-cement	120	—	4.75	—	0.21	
Wood, 16 in., 7.5 exposure	—	—	1.15	—	0.87	0.31
Wood, double, 16-in., 12-in. exposure	—	—	0.84	—	1.19	0.28
Wood, plus insul. backer board, 0.3125 in.	—	—	0.71	—	1.40	0.31
Siding						
Asbestos-cement, 0.25 in., lapped	—	—	4.76	—	0.21	0.24
Asphalt roll siding	—	—	6.50	—	0.15	0.35
Asphalt insulating siding (0.5 in. bed.)	—	—	0.69	—	1.46	0.35
Wood, drop, 1 × 8 in.	—	—	1.27	—	0.79	0.28
Wood, bevel, 0.5 × 8 in., lapped	—	—	1.23	—	0.81	0.28
Wood, bevel, 0.75 × 10 in., lapped	—	—	0.95	—	1.05	0.28
Wood, plywood, 0.375 in., lapped	—	—	1.59	—	0.59	0.29
Wood, medium density siding, 0.4375 in.	40	1.49	—	0.67		0.28
Aluminum or Steel, over sheathing						
Hollow-backed	—	—	1.61	—	0.61	0.29
Insulating-board backed nominal 0.375 in.	—	—	0.55	—	1.82	0.32
Insulating-board backed nominal 0.375 in., foil backed			0.34		2.96	
Architectural glass	—	—	10.00	—	0.10	0.20
Woods						
Maple, oak, and similar hardwoods	45	1.10	—	0.91	—	0.30
Fir, pine, and similar softwoods	32	0.80	—	1.25	—	0.33
0.75 in.	32	—	1.06	—	0.94	0.33
1.5 in.		—	0.53	—	1.89	
2.5 in.		—	0.32	—	3.12	
3.5 in.		—	0.23	—	4.35	

NOTES:

1. Resistance values are the reciprocals of C before rounding off C to two decimal places.
2. Conductivity varies with fiber diameter. Insulation is produced by different densities, therefore, there is a wide variation in thickness for the same R-value among manufacturers. No effort should be made to relate any specific R-value to any specific thickness. Commercial thicknesses generally available ran from 2 to 8.5.
3. Does not include paper backing and facing, if any.
4. Values are for aged board stock.
5. Insulating values of acoustical tile vary, depending on density of the board and on type, size and depth of perforations.
6. The U.S. Department of Commerce, Simplified Practice Recommendation for Thermal Conductance Factors for Preformed Above-Deck Roof Insulation, No. R 257-55, recognizes the specifications of roof insulation on the basis of the C-values shown. Roof insulation is made in thicknesses to meet the values.
7. Face brick and common brick do not always have these specific densities. When density is different from that shown, there will be a change in thermal conductivity.
8. Data on rectangular core concrete blocks differ from the above data on oval core blocks, due to core configuration, different mean temperatures, and possibly differences in unit weights. Weight data of the oval core blocks tested are not available.
9. Weights of units approximately 7.625 in. high and 15.75 in. long. These weights are given as a means of describing the blocks tested, but conductance values are all for 1 ft² of area.
10. Vermiculite, perlite, or mineral wool insulation. Where insulation is used, vapor barriers or other precautions must be considered to keep insulation dry.
11. Values for metal siding applied over flat surfaces vary widely, depending on amount of ventilation air space beneath the siding; whether air space is reflective or nonreflective;and on thickness, type, and application of insulating backing-board used. Values given are averages for use as design guides, and were obtained from several guarded hotbox tests (ASTM C236) or calibrated hotbox (BSS 77) on hollow backed types and types made using backing-boards of wood fiber, foamed plastic, and glass fiber. Departures of ± 50% or more from the values given may occur.

MAJOR APPLICATIONS FOR GENERIC INSULATION MATERIALS

MAJOR APPLICATIONS FOR GENERIC INSULATION MATERIALS

MAJOR APPLICATIONS	LOOSE FILL INSULATION					RIGID INSULATING BOARDS				
	Cellulose	Fiber Glass	Mineral Fiber	Perlite	Vermiculite	Mineral/Fiberglass	Cellular Glass	Cellular Plastics	Wood Fiber	Composite Foam/Mineral
INDUSTRIAL										
Roof/Ceiling										
Above Roof Deck						N-R	N-R	N-R	N-R	N-R
Below Roof Deck										
Walls										
In Cavities				N	N		N	N		
Sheathing or Siding						N-R	N-R	N-R	N-R	
Floors										
Concrete Slab							N-R	N		
Wood or Steel Joists								N-R		
COMMERCIAL										
Roof/Ceiling										
Above Roof Deck						N-R	N-R	N-R	N-R	N
Below Roof Deck	N-R									
Walls										
In Cavities	R			N	N		N	N		
Sheathing or Siding						N-R	N-R	N-R	N-R	
Floors										
Concrete Slab						N	N-R	N		
Wood or Steel Joists								N-R		
RESIDENTIAL										
Roof/Ceiling										
In-Frame Cavities	N-R	N-R	N-R	N-R	N-R	N				
Above Roof Sheathing								N-R	N	N
Cathedral Ceilings								N-R	N-R	N-R
Walls										
In-Frame Cavities	R	R	R	R		N				
Sheathing or Siding						N		N-R	N	
Floors										
Wood Joisted	N-R					N				
Concrete Slab										
Basement Wall										
Exterior						N		N		
Interior						N		N-R		

N – Used in New Construction; R – Used in Retrofitting

MAJOR APPLICATIONS FOR GENERIC INSULATION MATERIALS (Concluded)

MAJOR APPLICATIONS	INSULATING BATTS OR BLANKETS		FOAMED IN PLACE INSULATION		SPRAYED IN PLACE INSULATION		OTHER	
	FIBER GLASS	MINERAL FIBER	URETHANE FOAM	UREA BASED FOAM	CELLULOSE	MINERAL FIBER	INSULATING CONCRETE	REFLECTIVE INSULATION
INDUSTRIAL								
Roof/Ceiling								
Above Roof Deck	--	N-R	N-R	--	--	--	N-R	--
Below Roof Deck	N-R	N-R	R	--	N-R	N	--	N-R
Walls								
In Cavities	N-R	N-R	N-R	--	--	--	--	--
Sheathing or Siding	--	--	--	--	--	--	--	--
Floors								
Concrete Slab	--	--	--	--	--	--	N-R	--
Wood or Steel Joists	N-R	N-R	N-R	--	N	--	N-R	--
COMMERCIAL								
Roof/Ceiling								
Above Roof Deck	--	--	N-R	--	--	--	N-R	--
Below Roof Deck	N-R	N-R	R	--	N-R	N	--	--
Walls								
In Cavities	N-R	N-R	N-R	--	N	--	--	--
Sheathing or Siding	--	--	--	--	--	--	--	--
Floors								
Concrete Slab	--	--	--	--	--	--	N-R	--
Wood or Steel Joists	N-R	N-R	N-R	--	N	--	N-R	--
RESIDENTIAL								
Roof/Ceiling								
In-Frame Cavities	N-R	N-R	--	--	N	--	--	N
Above Roof Sheathing	--	--	N-R	--	N-R	--	--	--
Cathedral Ceilings	N-R	N-R	--	N-R	--	--	--	N
Walls								
In-Frame Cavities	N	N	N-R	N-R	N	--	--	--
Sheathing or Siding	--	--	--	--	--	--	--	--
Floors								
Wood Joisted	N-R	N-R	--	--	--	--	--	N-R
Concrete Slab	--	--	--	--	--	--	--	--
Basement Wall								
Exterior	--	N-R	--	--	--	--	--	--
Interior	N-R	N-R	--	--	--	--	--	N

N - Used in New Construction; R - Used in Retrofitting

GLOSSARY OF TERMS AND ABBREVIATIONS

British Thermal Units (BTU's)— A thermal measuring system based on the amount of heat necessary to raise the temperature of one pound of water 1 degree Fahrenheit (°F); a unit of heat approximating that given off by burning a wood kitchen match. 1 Ton of air conditioning = the removal of 12,000 BTU's; 1 BTU/min = 17.6 watts.

Coefficient of Heat Transmission or Thermal Transmittance (U)— A measurement of the conductive capacity of a material; the thermal transmission in unit time through a unit area of a particular body or assembly including its boundary films, divided by the difference between the environmental temperatures on either side of the body or assembly; the reciprocal of R-value (BTU/hrft^2 °F). The lower the U-value, the higher the insulating value of the assembly.

Condensation— the process of changing a vapor into a liquid by extracting heat from the vapor (water vapor requires the removal of about 960 BTU/lb).

Conductance, Thermal (C)— a measure of a material's ability to transmit heat through it by conduction; specifically, it is the amount of heat transferred in BTU's/hr through a designated thickness of a homogeneous or non-homogeneous material with an area of one square foot, when 1 °F temperature difference is maintained across the two sides (BTU/hrft^2 °F); the lower the (C), the higher the insulating value of the material (A 4" thick piece of material having a k-value of 0.8 will have a C-value of 0.2).

Conduction, Thermal— the movement of heat from molecule to adjacent molecule, through a substance or from one substance to another in contact with it.

Conductivity, Thermal (k)— Similar to thermal conductance, it is the measure of a 1 inch thick homogeneous material's ability to transmit heat; specifically, it is the amount of heat transferred in BTU/hr through a homogeneous 1 inch thick material with an area of one square foot when a 1°F temperature difference is maintained across the two sides (BTU/hrft^2 °F); the lower the (k), the higher the insulating value of the material.

Convection, Thermal— the transfer of heat energy by moving masses of matter, such as the circulation of a liquid or gas. This can occur from changes in density due to temperature differences or pressure.

Degree-day— a unit measuring the extent to which the outdoor mean (average) daily dry-bulb temperature falls below (in the case of heating) or rises above (in the case of cooling) an assumed base; the base, unless otherwise designated, is normally taken at 65°F for heating; one degree day is counted for each degree of difference below (for heating) or excess over (for cooling) the assumed base for each calendar day on which such deficiency or excess occurs.

Dew Point Temperature— the temperature at which condensation starts to form for a given humidity and pressure; this temperature corresponds to saturation (100% Relative Humidity).

Energy— the capacity for doing work; taking a number of forms which may be transformed from one into another, such as thermal (heat), mechanical (work), electrical, and chemical; in customary units it is measured in kilowatt-hours (kwh) or British Thermal Units (BTU's).

Envelope, Building— the protective shell of a building which separates the outside environment through which thermal energy may be transferred in or out.

Heat— a form of kinetic energy that flows from one body to another because of a temperature difference between them; the effects of heat result from the motion of molecules; heat is usually measured in Calories or British Thermal Units (BTU's).

Heat Capacity— a property of a material to absorb heat; the quantity of heat in BTU's needed to raise 1 cubic foot of the material 1°F.

Infiltration— the uncontrolled flow of air into or out of a building through cracks around windows and doors, other openings, and porous materials caused by differences in air pressure and/or density resulting from wind and/or temperature changes.

Insulation— any material with a high resistance to heat transmission (R) normally used to retard heat transfer in buildings.

Permeability— a property of a substance which permits passage of water vapor.

Perms (Permeance)— the ratio of water vapor transmission through a surface to the vapor pressure difference across that surface; permeance or perms is normally expressed in grains/(Sq ft) (Hr) per mercury vapor pressure difference.

Radiation or Radiant— the flow of energy across open space via electromagnetic waves such as visible light; the process in which energy in the form of rays of light and heat is transferred from body to body without heating the intermediate air acting as a transfer medium.

Relative Humidity (RH)— the ratio of water vapor in the air to the amount it could potentially hold at that given temperature.

Resistance, Thermal (R-value)— a measure of a material's resistance to the flow of heat; the unit time for a unit area of a particular body or assembly having defined surfaces with a unit average temperature difference established between the two surfaces per unit of thermal transmission; (hrft^2 °F/BTU); it is the reciprocal of the U-value or (1/BTU/hrft^2 °F); the higher the (R), the higher the insulating value of the material.

Specific Heat— the property of a material's ability to absorb heat; the quantity of heat, in BTU's, needed to raise the temperature of 1 pound of the material 1°F (specific heat for water=1 BTU/lb °F).

Temperature— the measurement of the level of motion or agitation of molecules and atoms with reference to the tendency to communicate heat to matter.

Thermal Mass or Inertia— the tendency of heavy materials used in construction to resist temperature change through their ability to store large quantities of heat; ability of materials to dampen or average significant daily temperature swings.

Vapor Barrier— a moisture resistant layer of material applied to the surface enclosing a space or building to prevent moisture penetration.

Ventilation— the process of supplying or removing air by a natural or mechanical means to or from a space.

ADDITIONAL ABREVIATIONS

ASHRAE— American Society of Heating, Refrigeration and Air Conditioning Engineers

ASTM— American Society for Testing Materials

BEPS— Building Energy Performance Standards

BOCA— Building Officials and Code Administrators

BUR— Built-up Roofing

CPSC— Consumer Product Safety Commission

DOE— Department of Energy

EPS— Expanded or Molded Polystyrene

ft or (') — Foot (Feet)

ft² or **SF** or **sq.'**— square foot (square feet)

ft³— cubic foot (cubic feet)

hr or **H**— Hour(s)

ICBO— International Conference of Building Officials

in or (")— inch(es)

lb— Pound(s)

OEM— Original Equipment Manufacturers

SBCC— Southern Building Code Congress

UFFI— Urea-Formaldehyde Foam Insulation

WVT or **WVP**— Water Vapor Transmission or Permeability (perm-in)